Free State   KwaZulu-Natal

Northern Cape

SOUTH AFRICA

Eastern Cape

WESTERN CAPE

72 73
74 75

TO COLESBERG / GARIEP DAM

TO SOMERSET EAST

Karoo National
Park   **N1**
59
58 ◉ **Beaufort West**

O   O

K A R

N12

KLEIN KAROO 106-107

N
Seweweekspoort
\◉ *Pass*   *Swartberg*
◉ *Pass*
62 *61*
'Route 62'   ◉ *Meiringspoort*
Schoemanspoort *Pass*
Oudtshoorn *61* *Pass* ◉

TO ADDO ELEPHANT PARK

T H E G A R D E N R O U T E
54 ◉ **George** *57* ◉ **56**
Outeniqua   ◉ *5757*
Choo-tjoe   **Knysna** **Plettenberg Bay**
55   Knysna
Dias Museum   Lagoon
55 ◉ **Mossel Bay** *56*
N2
GARDEN ROUTE 98-105

TO PORT ELIZABETH

66 67
68 69

MapStudio

First edition published in 2004 by Map Studio
www.mapstudio.co.za
0860 10 50 50

HEAD OFFICE
Cornelis Struik House
80 McKenzie Street
Cape Town
Tel: 021 462 4360

PO Box 1144
Cape Town, 8000

SALES OFFICES
Map Studio Johannesburg
7 Wessel Road, Rivonia
Tel: 011 807 2292

Map Studio Cape Town
Unit 7, M5 Freeway Park
Maitland
Tel: 021 510 4311

Map Studio Durban
Shop 3A, 47 Intersite Avenue
Umgeni Park
Tel: 031 263 1203

ISBN: 1 86809 662 9
10 9 8 7 6 5 4 3 2 1

Printed in Singapore by
Tien Wah Press (Pte)Ltd.

Photographic Credits:
Struik Image Library
t = top, c = centre, b = bottom.
Colour Library: 30t, 61right. **Chanan Weiss:** 10t&c, 45.
Shaen Adey: 3, 4-5, 12-13, 14b, 15-20, 22b, 23t, 24, 26b, 27, 29b, 31, 33, 40b, 41-42, 44, 47-48, 50, 52t, 56t, 57.
Dominic Barnardt: 11t&b. **Nigel J Dennis:** 59b
Gerhard Dreyer: 29b, 54-55, 56b. **Kristo Pienaar:** 35.
Jéan du Plessis: 9t. **Peter Pickford:** 9b, 11c, 39t.
Walter Knirr: 22t, 26t, 36-37, 46t, 60b.
Jacques Marais: 10b. **Keith Young:** 51t.
Erhardt Thiel: 14t, 23b, 25, 28, 40t, 52b, 62-63.
Hein von Horsten: 21, 29t, 34, 38, 46b, 51b, 58, 61left.
Lanz von Horsten: 30b, 49, 53.
South African National Library: 8b.
Iziko/William Fehr Collection: 8t.

Although every effort has been made to ensure that this guide is up to date and current at time of going to print, the Publisher accepts no responsibility or liability for any loss, injury or inconvenience incurred by readers or travellers using this guide.

Map Studio Tourist team
Dénielle Lategan
Edward Hill
Elaine Fick
Elmari Kuyler
John Loubser
Lois O'Brien
Mark Hedington
Maryna Beukes
Myrna Collins
Ryan Africa
Simon Lewis
Broderick Kupka (Sales: Johannesburg)
Gina Moniz (Sales: Cape Town / Durban)

Special thanks to Mariëlle Renssen, Leizel Brown and Cathy Martin for their contributions.

Been there, done that?
Please let us know if you find any interesting information on your travels through the Western Cape or notice any changes. We'll reward the 10 best contributions with a copy of this guide when we update.

Send your contributions to:
Simon Lewis
Map Studio Tourist
PO Box 1144
Cape Town 8000

or e-mail tourist@mapstudio.co.za

WESTERN CAPE

Western Cape

Western Cape W

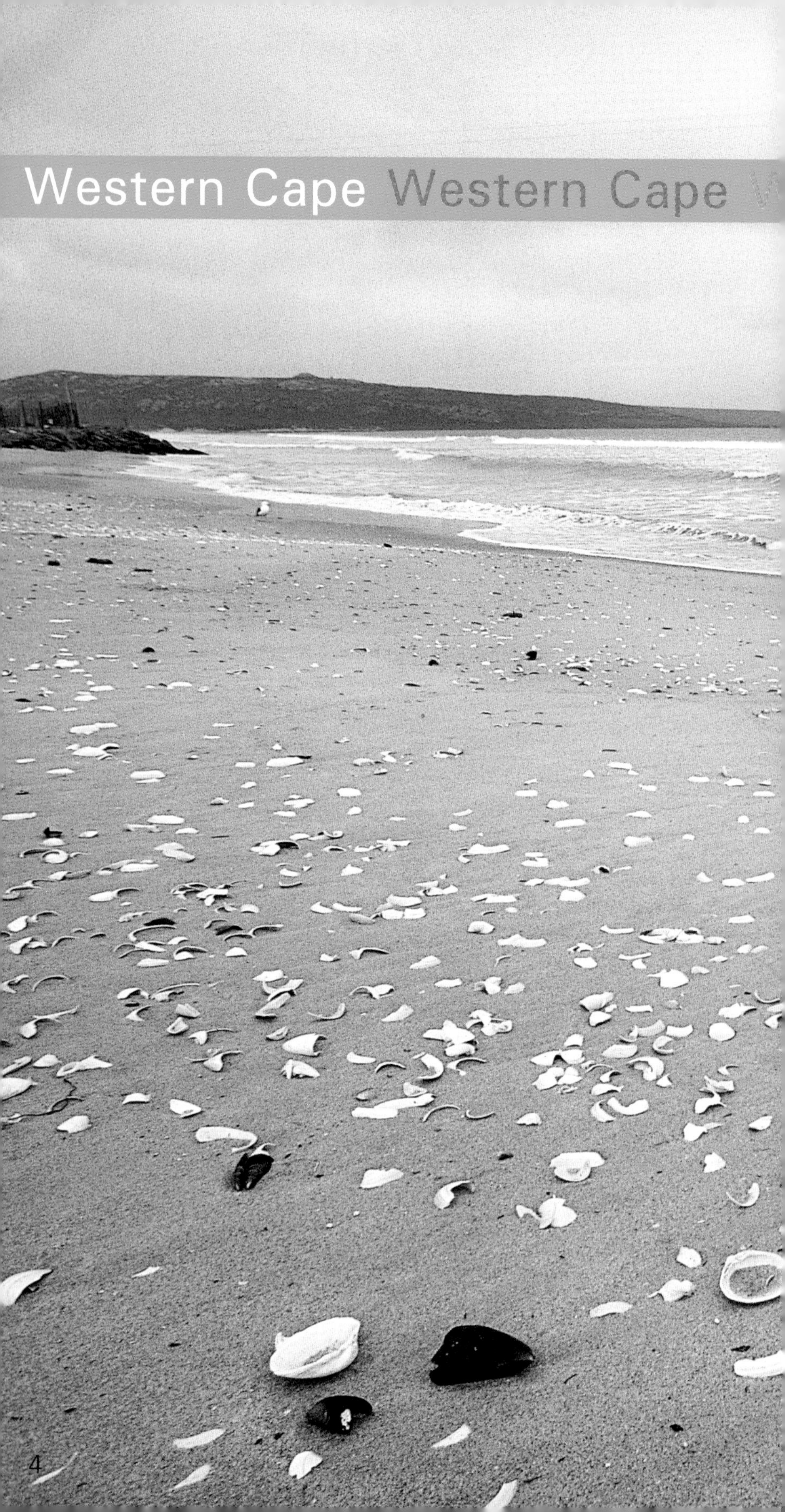

Covering two coastlines, the Western Cape enjoys massive geographical diversity, affording the area plenty of habitats, vegetation and landscapes.

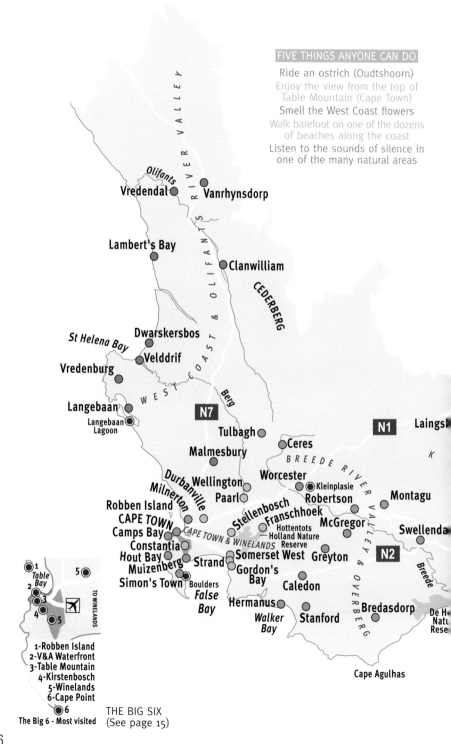

Ride an ostrich (Oudtshoorn)
Enjoy the view from the top of Table Mountain (Cape Town)
Smell the West Coast flowers
Walk barefoot on one of the dozens of beaches along the coast
Listen to the sounds of silence in one of the many natural areas

Olifants
Vredendal ● Vanrhynsdorp

OLIFANTS RIVER VALLEY

Lambert's Bay ●

Clanwilliam ●

CEDERBERG

St Helena Bay
Dwarskersbos ●
Velddrif ●

Vredenburg ●

Berg

Langebaan ●
Langebaan Lagoon

WEST COAST & OLIFANTS

N7

Tulbagh ●
Malmesbury ●

Ceres ●

N1   Laings

BREEDE RIVER VALLEY   K

Durbanville
Milnerton Wellington
Paarl ●
Worcester ●
Kleinplasie ●
Robertson ●

Montagu ●

Robben Island
CAPE TOWN
Camps Bay ●
Constantia ●
Hout Bay ●
Muizenberg
Simon's Town

CAPE TOWN & WINELANDS

Stellenbosch
Franschhoek
Hottentots-Holland Nature Reserve

McGregor ●

Swellenda

Strand
Somerset West Greyton ●
Gordon's Bay
Caledon ●

N2

BREEDE

OVERBERG

Boulders
False Bay

Hermanus ●

Walker Bay

Stanford ●

Bredasdorp ●

De H Natu Rese

Cape Agulhas

1
Table Bay
2
3
4   5
TO WINELANDS

5 ●

✈ TO WINELANDS

6

1-Robben Island
2-V&A Waterfront
3-Table Mountain
4-Kirstenbosch
5-Winelands
6-Cape Point

The Big 6 - Most visited

THE BIG SIX
(See page 15)

A floral paradise, some of the Western Cape's most revered species include ericas, proteas and the more elusive – and spectacular – disa.

Occupying the southern tip of the mega-continent, Africa, South Africa can match the best of them when it comes to contrasts in a single, unified land. 'Rainbow' nation? That it is, but not only in terms of its people; it is multi-hued also in terms of summer and winter, west coast and east coast, upland and lowland, mountain crest and shoreline. Of the nine provinces that glue together the jigsaw of this country's boundaries, Western Cape Province is arguably the one that attracts the most travellers and holiday-makers. The verdict depends on you, the visitors, to this green, fertile, river-dissected, rain-washed (and wind-blown) fruit- and bread-basket of South Africa. Climates in the Western Cape vary from the pretty-much rain-free and stony Namaqualand, to the truly Mediterranean hot-summer, rain-drenched-winter climate of Cape Town and its surrounds, up to the Garden Route's balmy, high-rainfall, temperate forest environs.

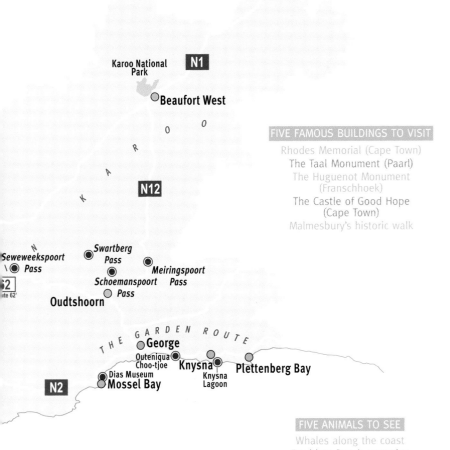

FIVE FAMOUS BUILDINGS TO VISIT

Rhodes Memorial (Cape Town)
The Taal Monument (Paarl)
The Huguenot Monument (Franschhoek)
The Castle of Good Hope (Cape Town)
Malmesbury's historic walk

FIVE ANIMALS TO SEE

Whales along the coast
Boulders Beach penguins
Loeries in Knysna
Cape Mountain Zebra in De Hoop Nature Reserve
Birds on the West Coast

FIVE NATURE RESERVES

Cape Peninsula National Park
Karoo National Park
West Coast National Park
De Hoop Nature Reserve
Cederberg Wilderness Area

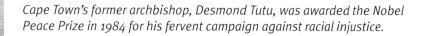

Cape Town's former archbishop, Desmond Tutu, was awarded the Nobel Peace Prize in 1984 for his fervent campaign against racial injustice.

Portrait of Jan van Riebeeck? Is this the real face of the founder of South Africa? The debate rages!

THE CAPE CULTURAL MIX

The earliest inhabitants of the southern tip of Africa were the San Bushmen, descendents of the Khoina peoples. Around 1000AD these Khoi-San were joined by migrating Bantu speakers who came from the north of the country. It was these cultural groups that Hollander Jan van Riebeeck encountered when his ship hit the shores of Table Bay. Today's Cape 'coloured' people are descended from the Khoina and the original Dutch settlers. After the arrival of the Dutch, newcomers to the fledgling colony arrived in the form of French and British settlers, as well as slaves and political refugees from Madagascar, Indonesia and Malaysia; indentured labourers from India later joined them. The British went on to make their mark after they took possession of the Cape permanently in 1806, leading to a major influx of British settlers in 1820.

A NEW COLONY ON THE WAY TO THE EAST

Cape Town began its lively existence in April 1652 as a halfway trading station. Lively? You have only to read the diaries of the genteel ladies who accompanied the early governors to gauge how the seeds of Cape Town's latent social merry-go-round were sown. 17-century traders of the Dutch East India Company, on their way to their colonies in the East, needed to replenish their fresh fruit and vegetable stores to stave off scurvy. The little settlement, headed up by its first Dutch commander, Jan van Riebeeck and his wife Maria de la Quellerie, soon swelled with the arrival (from 1688) of French Huguenots fleeing religious persecution in Europe. They penetrated inland of Table Bay, establishing themselves at the foot of a series of towering mountain ranges, where they tilled and terraced the fertile soils. Their enterprise was the halfway station's gain: their precious knowledge of the delectable juice of the vine laid the roots for the Cape's winelands.

THEN CAME THE BRITISH

The Dutch wielded their might for two centuries, but with the Netherlands' power declining towards the end of the 18th century, the British took the gap. The Cape became a Crown Colony in 1814 and self-government followed in 1872. Change came in 1910, when the four separate territories of the fledgling South Africa were unified, with the Cape colony becoming one of four official provinces. Cape Town was designated as the new nation's legislative capital, and retains this status to this day. South Africa was expelled from the Commonwealth (Apartheid) and became a republic in 1961.

Jan van Riebeeck met the local strandloper leader, Autshumao, when he landed in Table Bay to setup his Dutch refreshment station. Beads and trinkets were offered by the Dutch as a greeting.

In July 2003, Nelson Mandela turned 85 in a multi-day, countrywide celebration surrounded by children, an image he is constantly associated with.

ical Historical Historical Historic

APARTHEID ... A DIRTY WORD

This truly South African term (literally meaning 'apartness') was created after 1948 when racial discrimination laws were instituted by Dutch-born Hendrik Verwoerd, first as Minister of Native Affairs, and later as Prime Minister between 1958 and 1966 – the year he was assassinated. These laws prohibited mixed-race marriages, resulted in the loss of land and the establishment of separate living areas for non-white cultural groups, removed the right to a proper education and restricted movement through the need to carry identity passes based on racial classification.

SEEING THE LIGHT

South Africa imprinted itself on the world's psyche in February 1990 when State President FW de Klerk unbanned the black parties (ANC, PAC and the Communist Party) and released Nelson Mandela, up until then a high-profile political activist and founder of the ANC's military wing uMkhonte we Siswe. Mandela had been a prisoner of the state for 27 years since 1964, most of it spent on Robben Island. On 27 April 1994, with much rejoicing, South Africa voted the ANC into power (63% of the votes), and Nelson Mandela became the first black president of the 'New South Africa'. In 1999 Mandela stepped down, and was succeeded by the present president, Thabo Mbeki. Mandela remains the country's great hero.

A RAINBOW NATION AND ITS CONSTITUTION

Former Anglican Archbishop Desmond Tutu, whose archdiocese was the City of Cape Town from 1986 (he has since relinquished his archbishopric), described the people of the 'new' South Africa (a term liberally peppering modern-day lingo, whether social or political) as 'the rainbow people of God'. It stuck, and the term Rainbow Nation has been sewn into the fabric of this land. Cape Town was the setting for the formulation of South Africa's Constitution, recognised as one of the world's most progressive; its Bill of Rights, which outlaws any discrimination in terms of ethnic or social origin, language, religion, gender or sexual orientation, is one of the most enlightened in existence today.

THE CAPE: CRADLE OF MANKIND?

At the turn of our new century, archaeologists made a historic find on the shores of Langebaan Lagoon, along the Cape's West Coast region. Tracks, in the form of fossilised footprints, were discovered in an outcrop of rock, dating back 117,000 years and representing the oldest form of the anatomically modern human being, *Homo sapiens*. These are believed to reinforce the theory that Africa is the cradle of mankind.

Nelson Mandela, one of the world's best-known faces and a universal icon for freedom and the fight for democratic change.

THE PEOPLE AND THE LINGO

With the transition from a white autocratic government to a multi-party democracy in 1994, the country legislated 11 official languages – English, Afrikaans, and nine Bantu tongues (including Zulu, Xhosa, Sotho and Tswana). Cape Town has a population of roughly four million, made up of 57% Cape 'coloured', 24% white, 18% black (mainly Xhosa-speaking) and 1% Asian.

A San bushman, descendant of the Khoina. Small groups of these hunter-gatherers still eke out an existence in parts of Namaqualand and the Northern Cape today.

9

For any level of rock climbing, the Cape-based School of Mountaineering and the Mountain Club of SA will help you get to grips with the local terrain.

WALKS AND ROCK CLIMBS

It all starts on that great monolith that forces itself on everyone's psyche when they're in Cape Town: Table Mountain. There are innumerable routes on every face of this mountain that can be tackled on two feet; or with the aid of knees, toes and fingernails; or hanging suspended from a strong (you hope!) rope. Books, route pamphlets or Cape Town Tourism will direct you to the myriad options. Further afield of the mountain, Lion's Head and the Twelve Apostles, there is no lack of towering rockscapes to explore, starting in the Winelands region.

*Rock climbing (**top**) requires precision and pluck, while kloofing (**above**) is one giant leap of faith.*

HIKING AND KLOOFING

With so many mountains and valleys in Cape Town's backyard, there is a plethora of one- to eight-day hiking trails. Paths and routes are marked out through state reserves, private wilderness areas and small farms, many with basic overnight huts with minimal cooking and ablution facilities. Maps are provided with individual permits. Some of the best include the Otter, Tsitsikamma and Outeniqua trails, but if you like to get your feet wet, go kloofing in river valleys like Jonkershoek and Riviersonderend. Following the river, you can wade, boulder-hop and yell in primeval fashion while making a quantum leap into some of the mountain pools.

BIRD'S EYE VIEWS OF CITY- AND LANDSCAPES

When we say the world is your oyster, we mean it. Try a helicopter flip for size. Leaving from a helipad at the Waterfront, you'll see airborne perspectives of That Mountain, Cape Point or the Winelands that are guaranteed to change your worldview. Or you could drift over inland vine-terraces under the rainbow bubble of a hot-air balloon. If it's adrenaline you're seeking, the world of aero sports awaits you on the Cape's mountain heights, from Table Mountain to the Twelve Apostles, Lion's Head, Sir Lowry's Pass, Du Toit's Kloof Pass, and way beyond. Hang-gliders and para-gliders are constantly leaping off terra firma with wild abandon and, further inland, a small airfield base offers training courses for wannabe parachutists.

SPINNING ABOUT ON TWO WHEELS

Once again spoilt for choice with the Cape's mountain terrain, cyclists and mountain bikers have no cause to complain. In the more rugged wineland zones, a spider web of routes in the Breede River valley connect Worcester, Robertson and Montagu; the hot, dry Citrusdal landscape is freshened by the Olifants River and Cederberg mountains; De Hoop on the southern Cape coast has high dunes and wave-washed shores; and if you've had enough of blue skies, the Garden Route's hardwood forests around Kranshoek and Diepwalle Forest Station will give you plenty of branches to duck under and knobbly roots to fly over.

Mountain biking near Stellenbosch.

Capetonians have a wild imagination and have created numerous special-interest routes: flowers, crayfish, fruit, cheese (and wine!), wrecks and whales.

Big wave surfing at Dungeons, near Hout Bay.

BOUNCING ABOUT ON FOUR WHEELS

Word has it that some of the 4x4 trails laid out in the not-to-be-sneered-at Cape mountainscapes have rattled the most hardened of would-be Camel Man adventurers. The list of possibilities is endless: Montagu has the Langeberg range; Robertson, Greyton and McGregor the Riviersonderend mountains; Worcester and Ceres, the Hex River; Wellington, the Dutoitskloof mountains; while Stellenbosch and Somerset West boast the Helderberg and Hottentots Holland ranges. Penetrating into Karoo territory is the awe-inspiring Swartberg. Take your pick ... and hold your breath.

MESSING ABOUT IN H2O

Cape Town is not short of windy days, particularly when the southeaster blows into town. Windsurfers can jump waves at Muizenberg or Fish Hoek in False Bay, or skate across calmer surfaces on lagoons or inland bodies of water such as Seekoevlei, Rietvlei, Milnerton Lagoon or Langebaan. Kayakers, too, have the best of both worlds – miles and miles of west and east coast shoreline, or any one of the numerous protected lagoons. There are also multi-day organised expeditions, and plenty of local outfits who earn their keep by hiring out equipment and sharing their expertise.

FUN ON A WHITE-WATER RAFT

You can plunge into different degrees of white water (on a raft, of course) depending on the river and time of year. Multi-day expeditions on two- and eight-person inflatable rafts navigate sections of the Orange River (in the extreme north) and the Breede for wild-water running or quiet paddling, depending on your courage levels. This comes with experienced guides, equipment and great meals, while the evenings are spent under a canopy of stars. If you merely want to test the waters, the Breede offers a lazy Winelands canoe day-trip in the Worcester area, with historic homesteads, wine-tasting and riverbank picnics.

FROM ADRENALINE ...

If your ticker needs a little speed therapy, you won't be able to resist a steel cage dive in the cold, deep, offshore Cape waters to meet a Great White Shark eyeball-to-massive-eyeball. Attracted by bait trailed behind the boat, you'll be wetsuited and safely ensconced inside the cage while they thrash at the grub around you, *hopefully* remaining outside the cold steel bars.

... TO COMATOSE

After this, your idea of fun will almost certainly be to sink your butt onto something comfortable and let the world slip by. You could put that same butt into a saddle and go ambling along the eternally beautiful sugar-sands of Noordhoek Beach and be whispered to by the waves; or wander on horseback through leafy vines in the shadow of a jagged mountain skyline on a graceful wine farm. Alternatively, catch a steam train the old-fashioned way and huff and puff to Spier Estate for the day, or command a carriage on the Outeniqua Choo-Tjoe and be mesmerised by the way it clings precariously to the mountainside.

*Windsurfing (**below**) and kite surfing (**bottom**) are popular at Bloubergstrand beach, which is whipped by strong coastal winds.*

Cape Town is quick and easy to get around ... as long as you avoid rush hour traffic and can spot Table Mountain (locals tend to 'navigate' by the mountain).

Cape Town Cape Town Cape To

Africa being Africa (whopping distances across great undeveloped tracts and a not-so-developed transport infrastructure), you need your own vehicle if you'd like to do justice to your explorations. Beg, borrow or hire one – there's no need to steal, as there are plenty of car-hire companies operating at airports and in the major towns. It can't be ignored: mileage between major towns (and therefore between tourist sites), distances between scenic vistas, treks between windy and sheltered beaches, and even the hop from one watering hole to the next, simply can't be achieved on the existing bus and rail system. Yes, there is a pretty decent rail-line linking all of the Southern Suburbs' towns between Cape Town and Simon's Town; yes, round-trip buses ferry visitors between the city centre and the Waterfront area; and the 3-wheeled Rikki taxis can be called up at a moment's notice for short city-based trips. But this ain't gonna get you to Hout Bay and Chapman's Peak, Cape Point, the Winelands or up the West Coast to Namaqualand. Of course, there are many organised coach tours that will take you all the way up to the Garden Route and beyond – if that's the kind of trip that turns you on. So ... the choice is yours.

Top left: Minstrels in full dress.
Left: Touring bus on Signal Hill.

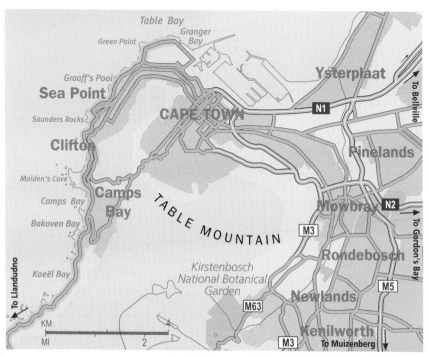

Cape Town is a cosmopolitan city with a wide range of architectural influences. Concrete fundis will enjoy her contemporary and unusual constructions.

THE BIG SIX

Cape Town is famous for many world-class attractions, but the Big Six of most-visited destinations is made up of the following:

Robben Island
Walk in Nelson Mandela's footsteps.
V&A Waterfront
Hop, shop and bop to your heart's content.
Table Mountain
Get an eyeful of Cape Town from the summit.

The Bo-Kaap is the seat of local Malay culture. Some homes date back to around 1810, and many feature ornate parapets and plasterwork.

Observatory Main Road is alive with spirit at night … witnessed by the lack of parking!

Kirstenbosch National Botanical Garden
Kick back and relax amidst the floral fragrances and rolling lawns.
Winelands
A powerful magnet for most tourists: great grapes and a fun day of estate-hopping.
Cape Point
Pristine beaches, fabulous fynbos and a dramatic and treacherous coastline washed by mighty waves.

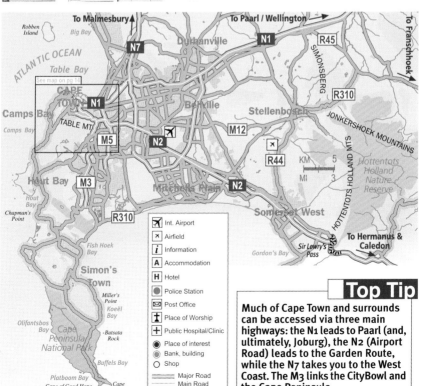

Int. Airport
Airfield
Information
Accommodation
Hotel
Police Station
Post Office
Place of Worship
Public Hospital/Clinic
Place of interest
Bank, building
Shop
Major Road
Main Road
Other Road

Top Tip

Much of Cape Town and surrounds can be accessed via three main highways: the N1 leads to Paarl (and, ultimately, Joburg), the N2 (Airport Road) leads to the Garden Route, while the N7 takes you to the West Coast. The M3 links the CityBowl and the Cape Peninsula.

Get cosmic and climb Lion's Head at Full Moon in summer: watch the yellow moonrise as the red sunsets. Unforgettable – just don't forget to take a torch!

Cape Town Cape Town Cape To

Table Mountain watches over the Waterfront.

Sandwiched between Table Bay and Table Mountain, the Atlantic prevents the city from expanding: mind you, land has already been reclaimed from the harbour to accommodate a growing metropolis that began life as Jan van Riebeeck's refreshment station. The city foreshore and ever-evolving V&A Waterfront complex are built on foundations that have been snatched back from the ocean.

NO TIME TO WASTE
If the Southeaster's not doing a Marilyn Monroe 'thang' on you, let the cableway (360° views from a revolving floor) whisk you to the top of the mountain in a couple of minutes; or walk up Long Street to marvel at the filigreed Victorian balconies and oddles of nightlife (lord it up in Kennedy's Cigar Bar). Trawl Greenmarket Square's umbrella'd cobblestones for anything from African masks to beaded trinkets. Make for the Whale Well at the Planetarium in the Company Gardens, where giant skeletons hang from the ceiling; be awed by the hi-tech projections of the Southern Hemisphere's night sky. Then it's time to be posh: high tea at the gently pink Grande Dame, the Mount Nelson.

The cable car completes another round trip.

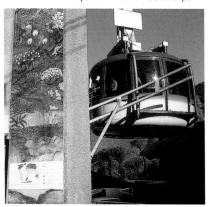

| Int. Airport |
| Airfield |
| Information |
| Accommodation |
| Hotel |
| Police Station |
| Post Office |
| Place of Worship |
| Public Hospital/Clinic |
| Place of interest |
| Bank, building |
| Shop |
| Major Road |
| Main Road |
| Other Road |

Every day at 12h00 (except Sundays) Signal Hill's canon fires off 1.5kg (3 lb) of gunpowder, scattering pigeons as the noongun's noise reverberates.

ape Town Cape Town Cape Town

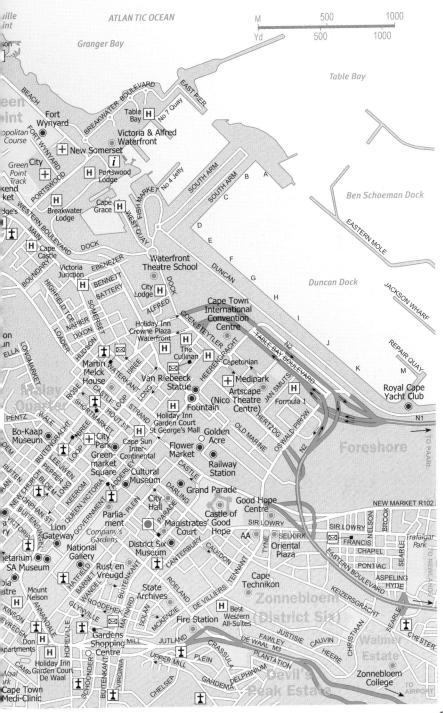

Bordjiesrif and Buffels Bay on the Cape of Good Hope's craggy coastline are lovely picnic and barbecue sites, nestling a toe's dip from the waves.

Scenic view of the Cape Peninsula.

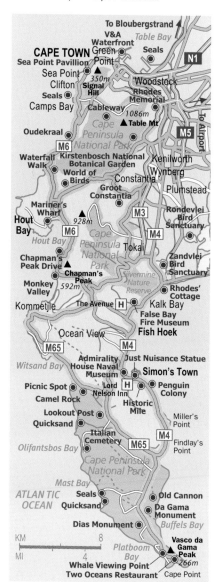

A 'TWEET' FOR ALL AGES

A visit to the World of Birds (on your way to Hout Bay and Chapman's Peak) is always a pleasure. This rehabilitation centre now has around 450 different species. Observe at your leisure (and sometimes from frighteningly close distances) Scarlet Ibis, Blue Crane, a flock of flamingoes and Egyptian Vultures. If you're brave you can eyeball some quizzical owls in the walkthrough cages: it's just you and the owls, so walk s-l-o-o-o-w! There are also porcupines, tortoises, marmosets, meerkats and monkeys to entertain and amuse the whole family.

GET TO THE POINT ... CAPE POINT

In the Cape of Good Hope (which forms part of the Cape Peninsula National Park) you're advised to roll up your windows against the chacma baboons, but keep your eyes peeled for eland, bontebok and other bokke. At the parking area, the lazy ones can take the funicular, while the energetically inclined can walk to the view site to see Cape Point being battered by wild and restless seas. The Two Oceans restaurant here has stupendous views across False Bay, and there's an excellent new visitors centre near the Dias Monument.

TABLE MOUNTAIN AND KIRSTENBOSCH

If you're of the fit-'n-active persuasion, thumb your nose at the cable car and tackle one of the myriad Table Mountain paths (easy *and* difficult) to the top, where the reservoirs are pretty and the views glorious. Kirstenbosch Botanical Garden offers you the birds and the bees – oh, and a massive array of trees and plants, not least of which is the lofty baobab in the glass conservatory. Rest ... and then 'do lunch' in the floor-to-ceiling-windowed restaurant. The Gardens also act as an outdoor art gallery, with scores of modern African sculptures decorating the lawns and flowerbeds.

Dias Monument, Cape Point.

The Cape Peninsula's coastline was feared by ancient mariners:
the list of wrecked and beached ships is lengthy ... and getting longer.

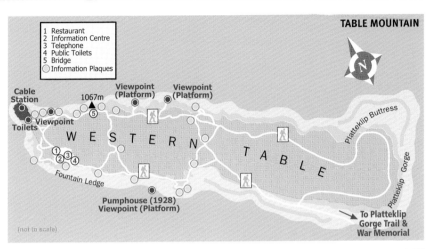

TABLE MOUNTAIN

1 Restaurant
2 Information Centre
3 Telephone
4 Public Toilets
5 Bridge
○ Information Plaques

Cable Station
Toilets
Viewpoint
1067m
Viewpoint (Platform)
Viewpoint (Platform)

W E S T E R N
T A B L E

Fountain Ledge

Platteklip Buttress
Platteklip Gorge

Pumphouse (1928)
Viewpoint (Platform)

To Platteklip
Gorge Trail &
War Memorial

(not to scale)

- ✈ Int. Airport
- ✈ Airfield
- *i* Information
- A Accommodation
- H Hotel
- ● Police Station
- ✉ Post Office
- ✝ Place of Worship
- ✛ Public Hospital/Clinic
- ● Place of interest
- ═══ Major Road
- ─── Main Road
- ┄┄┄ Other Road

Right: *Viewpoint on top of Table Mountain.*

KIRSTENBOSCH

Reservoirs
Fynbos Walk
Nursery Stream
Skeleton Stream
Window Stream

Proteas
Buchus
Proteas
Ericas
Fynbos Walk

Braille Trail
Smuts Track

Education Centre
Lecture Hall
Garden Centre
Parking

Cycads
The Koppie

Colonel Bird's Bath
Useful Plants
Pearson's Grave
Medicinal Plants
Fragrance Garden

Public Toilets
Water-wise Garden

Pearson's House

Mathew's Rockery
Vygies
Pond

Peninsula Garden
Vlei Garden

NBI Head Office

To Cape Town

Seed Orchard
Restios
Van Riebeeck's Hedge

Concert Stage
Annuals
MAIN GATE

Restaurant
Sculpture Garden

Parking
Toilets

Church of the Good Shepherd

To Hout Bay

Conservatory
Visitors' Centre

RYCROFT GATE
RHODES DRIVE M63
Parking
Nursery (no entry)
Curator's Office
RHODES DRIVE M63

(not to scale)

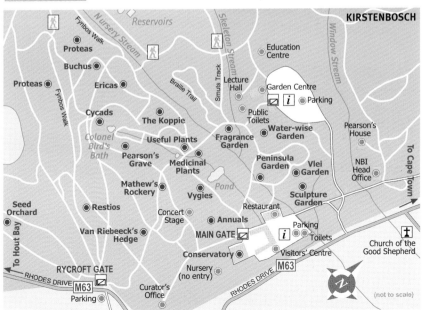

19

V&A Waterfront V&A Waterfron

It was Queen Victoria's son Prince Alfred who set into motion the building of Alfred Basin when he tumbled a load of rocks into the excavated sea floor of stormy Table Bay. Today, the Victoria and Alfred basins have morphed into the inexorably growing V&A Waterfront complex, a place for singing, laughing, drinking and eating – like that 'accessible' Graça wine. You can also do lots of shopping in chi-chi designer stores.

If you need some escapism from all this fun (more likely, if the credit card's maxed-out!), the IMAX movie theatre has a 5-storey screen with wraparound, multi-speaker digital sound. Immerse yourself in a world of absolutes: the highest peak, largest sea mammal, man-eating cats, the world's hottest spot – or the iciest. For a little excitement, test your nerves before the shatterproof glass, 2-million-litre Predator Tank at the Two Oceans Aquarium. A glass-width away from the serrated jaws of ragged-tooth sharks, you can see yourself reflected back in their cold emotionless gaze. At specific times, it's feeding time at the zoo when divers in chain mail brave the tank to satiate the ferocious fishies' appetites. Don't miss it. Finish the day with sundowners on the terrace of the

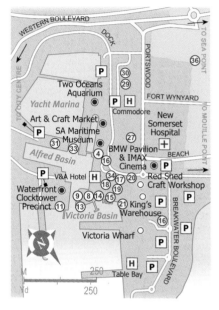

Radisson Hotel in next-door Granger Bay – crashing waves, swooping gulls, pastel skies and catamarans gliding out to sea on a zephyr's breath. It's tough in Africa.

Nelson Mandela Gateway in the V&A Waterfront.

1-Two Oceans Aquarium	15-Quay Four
2-Art & Craft Market	16-Buses to the City
3-SA Maritime Museum	17-Vaughan Johnson's
4-Dock Road Complex	Wine Shop
5-Robinson Graving Dock	18-Union Castle House
6-Alfred Basin	(Telkom Exploratorium)
7-V&A Hotel and Alfred Mall	19-Market Square
8-Pierhead	20-Ferryman's Tavern
9-Old Port Captain's Building	21-Agfa Amphitheatre
10-Clocktower Square	22-Victoria Wharf
11-Carradines	23-King's Warehouse
12-Victoria Basin	24-Red Shed Craft
13-Penny Ferry	Workshop
14-National Sea Rescue	25-BMW Pavilion & IMAX
Institute	Cinema

26-New Somerset Hospital	
27-Portswood Lodge	
28-Portswood Square	
29-UCTGraduate School of	
Business	
30-Breakwater Lodge	
31-Cape Grace Hotel	
32-Table Bay Hotel	
33-Bascule Bridge	
34-Waterfront Visitors	
Centre	
35-Seal Landing	
36-Green Point Stadium	

A historical and ecological heritage site today (its seabird breeding colony is protected and in 1999 it was declared a World Heritage Site), Robben Island was named after its seal population (seals are 'robbe' in Dutch). But it started its life as something much more sinister – it was a penal settlement as early as 1658, when Jan van Riebeeck banished his interpreter here. Under a more modern government it became a maximum-security prison in 1964, but its last political prisoners were all released in 1991.

Robben Island is most famous for the barred hole-in-the-wall of Nelson Mandela's cell, behind which, in 1963, he was condemned to remain for 18 of his 23-year sentence. And it is in the island's blinding white lime quarries that Mandela's eyesight suffered early damage – prison inmates were forced to work there for six hours a day.

Today, visitors are treated to a genuine first-hand account of life behind those forbidding walls through the eyes of ex-political inmates, who conduct a guided tour of the prison cells. A bus trip takes visitors to the quarry and other sites of interest around the island.

The prison on Robben Island.

The 3-hour Robben Island round-trip is very popular and bookings are made at the Robben Island Museum, V&A Waterfront (book well in advance – preferably days!).

Top Tip

Among these is the 18m-high (59ft) lighthouse, built in 1863 to replace the fire beacons once used to warn off sailors being tossed about on the high seas; its beam can be spotted 25km (16 miles) away.

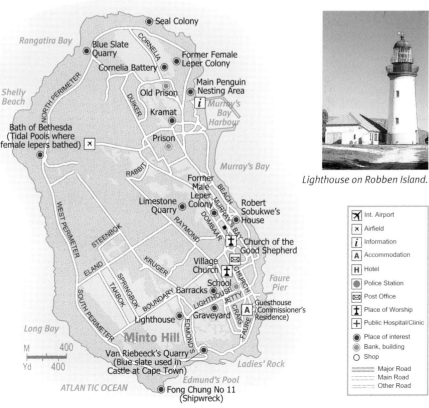

Lighthouse on Robben Island.

Map labels:

Seal Colony
Rangatira Bay
Blue Slate Quarry
CORNELIA
Former Female Leper Colony
Cornelia Battery
Main Penguin Nesting Area
Shelly Beach
NORTH PERIMETER
DUIKER
Old Prison
i Murray's Bay Harbour
Kramat
Bath of Bethesda (Tidal Pools where female lepers bathed)
Prison
RABBIT
Murray's Bay
WEST PERIMETER
Former Male Leper Colony
BEACH
Robert Sobukwe's House
Limestone Quarry
RAYMOND
DOMBAAR
MURRAY'S BAY
Church of the Good Shepherd
STEENBOK
ELAND
KRUGER
Village Church
Faure Pier
SPRINGBOK
TAKBOK
BOUNDARY
School
Barracks
CHURCH
LIGHTHOUSE
JETTY
Guesthouse (Commissioner's Residence)
SOUTH PERIMETER
Lighthouse
Graveyard
CRAIG
FAURE
EDMOND'S
Long Bay
Minto Hill
M 400
Yd 400
Van Riebeeck's Quarry (Blue slate used in Castle at Cape Town)
Ladies' Rock
ATLANTIC OCEAN
Edmund's Pool
Fong Chung No 11 (Shipwreck)

Legend:

✈	Int. Airport
✕	Airfield
i	Information
A	Accommodation
H	Hotel
●	Police Station
✉	Post Office
✝	Place of Worship
✚	Public Hospital/Clinic
●	Place of interest
◉	Bank, building
○	Shop
═══	Major Road
───	Main Road
----	Other Road

Milnerton's beaches are racked by the strong Cape Doctor (the south-easter) ... not great for sandy picnics, but loved by scores of wind- and kite-surfers.

Milnerton Milnerton Milnerton M

Another gorgeous Cape day ends in Milnerton.

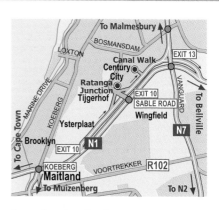

Stark, rocky and windswept, the West Coast has a unique beauty. Marine Drive (the M14) is a scenic route of dunes and sea that links Milnerton, Bloubergstrand and Melkbosstrand. Enjoy the best views of Table Mountain from Milnerton or Blouberg Beach.

CANAL WALK
Step into another world at Century City, sprawled alongside the N1 some 12km (7 miles) from the city centre. Built along a canal complete with rowboats, giant cupolas, painted murals and gilded columns decorate

the malls – it's all a bit like the Wizard of Oz on 'E'. Upmarket shopping, a games arcade for the kids, a cinema complex and a fast food 'hall' and entertainment area will appease rumbling tums. A large stage and entertainment area ajoins the food hall, with dozens of TV sets to entertain patrons.

RATANGA JUNCTION
The country's first full-scale theme park, Ratanga Junction will keep the kids out of your hair for hours. Launch them on 'jungle' cruises, a tube ride through the thrilling Crocodile gorge – or let them make like apes on the 18.5m (60ft) log-flume drop down Monkey Falls. If they have any nerves left, they can hit the pièce de résistance, the spine-chilling roller-coaster loops of the Cobra allow you to see the world at high speed – and from another perspective (upside down). Beware: ride queues can be LONG!

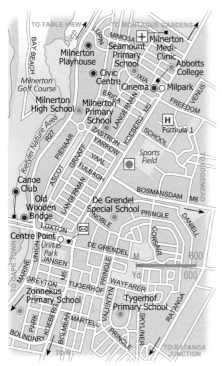

Canal Walk is flanked by a moat with boats for casual paddling after a heavy shopping trip!

On a rock pinnacle at one edge of Hout Bay beach is a statue of a leopard – a reminder of the sleek cats that once roamed the mountain slopes.

CAMPS BAY ▶

Cape Town's so-called Riviera – yes, France isn't the only country to have one – is where the rich people (and those who aspire to richness) play. It has palms, castor-sugar sands, pink sunsets, and is lined with terraced cafés and bars. They are the haunts of the scantily clad, sarong-enrobed young things in Gucci shades with mobile phones permanently attached to their ears. It's the place for bodacious curves and rippled, washboard stomachs. At sunset, trendoids hang out on the balcony of Blues Restaurant with something chilled in their hand to watch the sun sink behind the palm fronds, then move inside to try out the fusion cuisine served by eye-candy waitrons. If you're simply playing at being wealthy, find a secluded spot on the boulders at the beach and bid the sun farewell with your own bottle of sparkling wine.

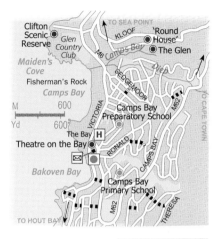

View of Lion's Head from Camps Bay beach.

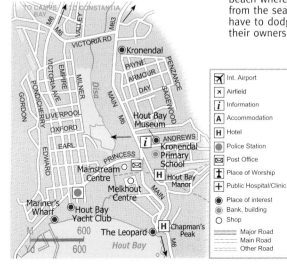

▐ Top Tip

In summer, Chapman's Peak Hotel is famous for its lobster, served as part of a giant mixed seafood platter and served on a balcony with great sea-views.

HOUT BAY ▼

If your yen is fish and chips eaten on unpretentious wooden benches with a harbour view, then Mariner's Wharf is for you (and the fish is so fresh you can almost taste the sea). This seafood bistro and fresh-fish market is built around Hout Bay's fishing harbour, with a beautifully placed curve of beach to the left and, to the right, a dockside for tourist cruises headed for Duiker Island to see the Cape fur seal colony. Work off your lunch with a stroll along the pretty beach where the mountains seem to rise from the sea; if it's late afternoon, you'll have to dodge the boisterous dogs taking their owners for a walk.

Cape fur seal.

✈	Int. Airport
✕	Airfield
i	Information
A	Accommodation
H	Hotel
●	Police Station
✉	Post Office
✝	Place of Worship
✚	Public Hospital/Clinic
●	Place of interest
◉	Bank, building
○	Shop
▬▬	Major Road
═══	Main Road
────	Other Road

23

Let a horse negotiate the pristine, mobile sands on Noordhoek's 6km (4-mile) beach while you relax in the saddle. Beware: the sea is treacherous!

Muizenberg Muizenberg Muizenberg M

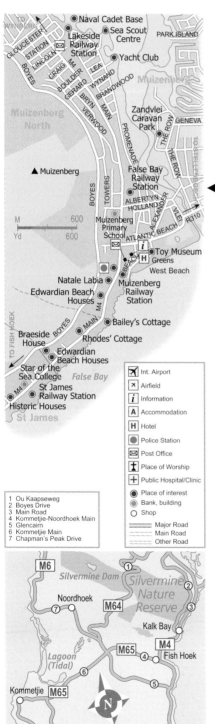

Beach huts on St James beach.

MUIZENBERG

Lined by now-shabby façades of once-grand beach mansions, Muizenberg is best known for its 40km (25-mile) sweep of powder-sand cradling False Bay all the way to the Strand. Surfers learn about balance on its long rollers, swimmers love the 5°C difference in sea temperature from Clifton. Release the child in you; catch the train that snakes along the sea line from Muizenberg to Simon's Town and poke your head out the window to catch the wind in your face.

KALK BAY

If the magpie in you can't resist bric-a-brac and glitter, they'll have to prise you away from the antique stores and art and craft shops lining Kalk Bay's main street. The Olympia Bakery will tempt you with the toasty, yeasty, crusty smells wafting out the door: it's so popular you have to chalk your name on the board and wait outside! Or lunch at Cape to Cuba, where trains thunder past while you're being served by pony-tailed waiters in berets.

Fishing boats in Kalk Bay's harbour.

Map legend:

1 Ou Kaapseweg
2 Boyes Drive
3 Main Road
4 Kommetjie-Noordhoek Main
5 Glencairn
6 Kommetjie Main
7 Chapman's Peak Drive

✈ Int. Airport
✈ Airfield
ℹ Information
A Accommodation
H Hotel
● Police Station
✉ Post Office
✝ Place of Worship
✚ Public Hospital/Clinic
● Place of interest
◉ Bank, building
○ Shop
━━━ Major Road
━━━ Main Road
━━━ Other Road

Top Tip

A drive (or run) along the winding Boyes Drive offers magnificent views of Muizenberg en route to Kalk Bay.

Penguins have an enviable libido and breed all year-round. A large appetite for pilchards and anchovies explains why they're busting out of their tuxedos.

Penguins at Boulders Beach.

SIMON'S TOWN ▼

The Navy has been in Simon's Town's blood since the 1700s, and since 1957 it's been the South African naval base. If history's your bag, a guided historical tour from the rail station to the Martello Tower takes in, among others, a museum housed in The Residency (1777) – the town's oldest building, it features a World War II pub – the Warrior Toy Museum (boys will be boys), and the naval museum. A story to tug at your heartstrings is that of Just Nuisance, a Great Dane ship's mascot who so inveigled himself into British soldiers' hearts that he was formally enrolled in the Navy as an Able Seaman. He was given a full military funeral, wrapped in the White Ensign; 200 seamen attended. Don't miss his bronze statue in Jubilee Square, in the heart of the town.

BOULDERS ▲

Just past Simon's Town, at Boulders Beach, a family of African Penguins (formerly called "Jackass" Penguins) has moved in. There are now several thousand thanks to a bit of healthy breeding! Elevated boardwalks have been built so visitors can get up-close and personal, which you'll find yourself doing with childlike abandon. The penguins look back quizzically from every crevice, watching the world walk by.

Simon's Town street scene.

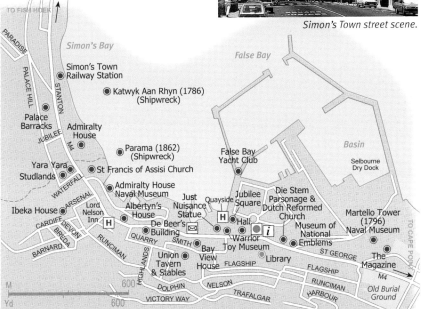

The popular Brandy Route (not as well-known as the 365-day-a-year Wine Route) leads to some of the world's oldest and largest brandy cellars.

WINELANDS

It's this part of the Western Cape Province that brings out the superlatives. How do you compete with towering jagged mountains, one range giving way to another, and many carrying whimsical names like Hex ('witch'), Drakenstein ('dragon stone') and Riviersonderend ('river with no end')? At their foot are tightly manicured vine terraces – and to cap it all, the eternally graceful curved and moulded gables of historical manor houses, a heritage left behind by early Dutch settlers. Passes forged through this mountain barrier to the east made it a gateway to the rest of the country. A region that, early on, was baptised the 'overberg', meaning 'over (or across) the mountains'. The Western Cape's winelands are the main reason for South Africa's plum position as seventh-largest wine producer in the world. A constantly mushrooming number of estates presently stand in the 90s; there are just fewer than 70 co-operatives and over 100 private cellars. The wineland areas are accessed via two major national routes, the N1 and N2, with multiple connecting and well-signposted principal roads. Crossing the mountains to the Overberg – and the 'southern' Cape region – the seaside summer 'play-zone' of Hermanus is king of whale-watching capitals. It has succeeded in turning Whale Season into a major festival.

CONSTANTIA ▶

The official Constantia Wine Route is limited to five estates – but dynamite comes in small packages! You will succumb to leafy oaks, whitewashed gables, vine-terraces and soaring mountains so close you could touch them (well, almost). Buitenverwachting, Groot Constantia, Klein Constantia and Constantia Uitsig all formed (at one time) part of a farm granted to Simon van der Stel in 1685. Groot Constantia offers the most bang for your buck in historic terms, with its old coach house, the Cloete wine cellar (now a wine museum), the manor house (converted into a 17th-century museum) and the Jonkershuis, now a restaurant. If, like Bacchus, you're into nectar of the gods, nearby Klein Constantia still produces Vin de Constance, a sweet wine from Muscat de Frontignac (get your tongue around that one!). Still made in the 18th-century tradition, this wine has seduced the taste buds of Napoleon, Bismarck and even Jane Austen. In the neighbourhood, Steenberg Estate (visits by appointment!) is also producing some memorable fermented juice from the vine.

Left: *Farm workers pluck truckloads of grapes from the vast vineyard estates.*
Bottom: *Vines, clear skies and mountain ranges stretch as far as the eye can see ...*

26

Slave bells were a symbol of power for the estate owner in bygone days. The bell was used to regulate the lives and working day of 'wine slaves'.

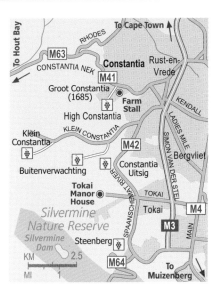

The slave bell at Altydgedacht wine estate, on the Durbanville Wine Route.

very respectable grapes that are being pressed in turn into highly quaffable wines. Durbanville Hills winery waves its magic wand with some very fine lemon-butter chardonnays and grassy-nosed sauvignon blancs ('sav blanc' and 'chard' to the wine toff). Diemersdal, Nitida, Meerendal and Altydgedacht don't do too badly either on all lip-smacking scores – red and white.

Top: *Buitenverwachting homestead looks out across a sea of vines.*
Above: *Groot Constantia's triangle gable.*

DURBANVILLE WINE ROUTE ▶
Durbanville is the upper crust (read: monied) residential and shopping mecca of Cape Town's Northern Suburbs – and settled into undulating hills and mountains, it puts on a pretty face, too. With the surrounding slopes clothed in vines, these are producing

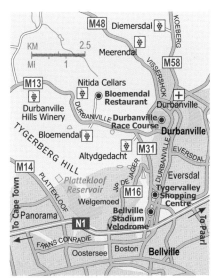

Oom Samie se Winkel is an old-fashioned village store crammed with collectables, artefacts of bygone years, chunky preserves and basketry.

SEAT OF LEARNING

Its streets lined with leafy oaks, this pretty university town's buildings rub shoulders with historical cottages and restored Cape Dutch, Cape Georgian, Regency and Victorian houses. Dorp Street is a marvel for its meticulously preserved façades, lined up like toy soldiers, and most of them historical monuments. You'll have built up a thirst from walking – Dorp is a l-o-o-o-n-g street – so it'll be necessary to make a dent on the students' famous local, De Akker. Stellenbosch also buys into café society, and there's a good selection of trendy coffee shops spilling out onto the pavement. If this is all too lowbrow for you, the university town has some good art galleries and art museums: Dorp Street Gallery, the gallery at 34 Ryneveld Street and the Rembrandt van Rijn Art Gallery.

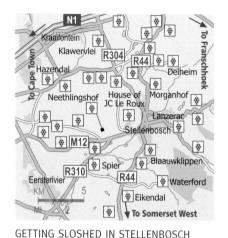

GETTING SLOSHED IN STELLENBOSCH

You can only visit three or four cellars in a day before you completely fall over, let alone follow the white lines on the road. You also obviously need to build in time to stop for lunch. At last count there were around 30 cellars and co-ops on four major roads within a 12km (7-mile) radius from Cape Town, so choose wisely. Delheim has atmosphere: low-lit, brick-arched wine cellar with wooden tables and benches; Morgenhof has a formal French-style garden and a tasting room with floor-to-ceiling views; Blaauwklippen is a working farm with vintage coaches, carriages and offering a coachman's platter for lunch.

Oom Samie se winkel: Time-Warp City.

Cabrière's Achim von Arnim will utterly charm you as he deftly lops off the necks of Pierre Jourdan wine bottles with a sabre (sabrage in French).

Late afternoon winter vineyards, snow-capped mountain peaks ... it's red wine time.

Franschhoek is a den for hedonists. Here you can party-party! Taking its cue from the French, it's a centre for wining and dining, festivals and fun. Year-round, the town stages festivals celebrating olives, cheese, grapes ... and the cherry on top is Bastille Day. For wine farms to visit, the graciously gabled L'Ormarins overlooks an ornamental pond and has a low, wooden-beam-ceilinged tasting room; La Motte's medieval-like long table and high-backed chairs look through glass panelling onto an oak-barrelled maturation cellar; Môreson, part of a working farm, has a large airy restaurant and a pretty terrace; and Haute Provence gives you superb wines in utterly gracious surrounds.

Top Tip

Sip chilled wine on the lawns at La Petite Ferme and take in the most stupendous view; then move onto the terrace for their smoked trout with horseradish sauce.

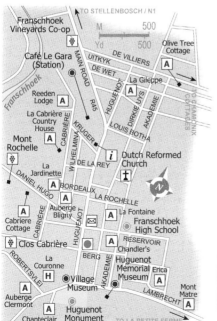

✈	Int. Airport
✕	Airfield
i	Information
A	Accommodation
H	Hotel
●	Police Station
✉	Post Office
✝	Place of Worship
✚	Public Hospital/Clinic
●	Place of interest
●	Bank, building
○	Shop
	Major Road
	Main Road
	Other Road

Franschhoek Vineyards Co-op.

Paarl's name comes from the Dutch, peerlbergh (pearl mountain), after explorer Abraham Gabbena spotted three smooth granite domes post-rain.

The Taal Monument will get tongues wagging.

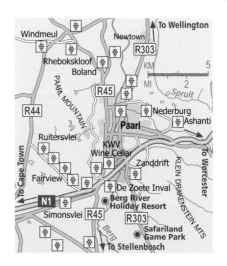

The Main Street in Paarl, which tails the Berg River, runs an amazing 11km (7 miles) and boasts rows of 18th- and 19th-century Cape Dutch and Georgian houses. About one-fifth of the country's total wine production comes from Paarl, and the most striking symbol of its wine history is La Concorde,

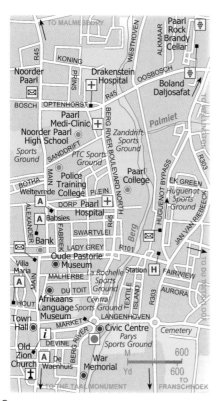

a Neo-Classical building with a sculpted pediment, dating back to 1956.

Don't make any detours round Fairview Wine Estate with its lip-smacking wines at lip-smacking prices. Watch the farm's Saanen (Swiss) goats nimbly navigating a thin spiral ramp up a tall tower, and then test their milk cheeses, some rolled in herbs or black pepper ... but the garlic cheese stand apart! At Zanddrift you can taste wines in a stone chapel that was built in the early 1940s by Italian prisoners of war. Nederburg, whose exquisite manor house has been captured by the click of many a camera lens, is internationally famous for its annual wine auction, and its auctioneer, Brit Patrick Grubb.

The swooping white spires on the hill are part of the Taal (or 'language') Monument, a tribute to the Afrikaans *taal*, it has three domes and three small pillars that vary in size and height. Nearby, Paarl Mountain can be climbed with the help of chain handholds. This granite outcrop, the world's second largest after Australia's Uluru, wears its age well – 500 million years and counting.

Paarl Rock, second in size only to Ayers Rock.

Wellington is known for its fresh-pressed olive oil (grown in the area), tanning industry and leather products (shoes, belts, handbags ... even couches!).

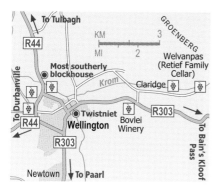

20 green bottles waiting for wine at Welgegund estate in Wellington.

WELLINGTON

Wellington is the headquarters of South Africa's dried fruit industry – you *must* taste the *mebos*, a sour-sweet chewy-fruity taste explosion. Inevitably, it's always the wine that draws the bees to the honey ... although Wellington still has to prove itself in the elegant wine stakes due to its dry, sunbaked climate. It also has its share of manor houses, among them Twistniet, the original homestead around which the town was built. The greatest stir is caused by Bain's Kloof Pass (northeast of the town via the R303 highway), 30km

(19 miles) of spectacular rock, sky and views. After the picnic spot at the summit, the pass drops to the Breede River valley where ravines, waterfalls and dramatic rock formations are your travel companions. Take your hat off to the pass builders, Andrew Geddes Bain and his son, Thomas. The interior, beyond these craggy mountains, was virtually impassable before the Bains arrived armed with their pickaxes. In winter, the peaks flanking Wellington often slap on their pretty snow-dusted aprons.

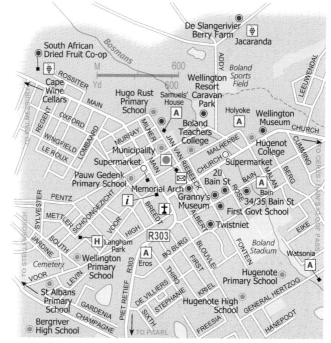

31

On Wednesdays and Saturdays a steam train leaves Cape Town at 9:30am, stopping at Spier (it has its own station), and returning in the afternoon.

Classic Wine Estates Classic Wi

GROOT CONSTANTIA ▶

The manor house (1685) is today a museum of authentic 17th-century life filled with paintings, furniture and *objets d'art*. On its gable (sculpted by Anton Anreith) rests the figure of Abundance, a more recent addition. If all this history is way too much for you, the Cloete wine cellar holds some gorgeous old drinking vessels and implements of torture once used for winemaking. No-one said touring was easy, so rest up in the Jonkershuis to sample traditional Cape Malay fare. 'Jonker' used to describe an estate owner's elder, bachelor son who generally had his own house on the estate. You can also choose to picnic under 300-year-old oak, chestnut, olive and banana trees.

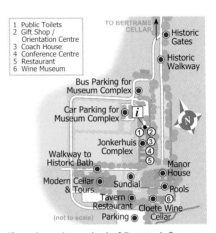

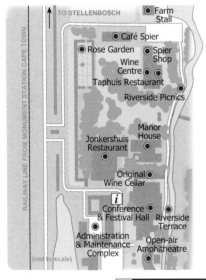

if you haven't yet tired of Eastern influences, the tables at the Jonkershuis groan delectably under the weight of an Indonesian and Cape Malay buffet.

BOSCHENDAL ▼

The ace in this estate's pack of cards is its H-shaped manor house, built in 1812 in the graceful Flemish style. Authentically furnished, from its cow-dung-washed kitchen floor to its wooden-beamed rafters, it's crammed with 18th-century treasures. One of the rooms holds a Dutch long-case clock (made in 1748) whose face shows the date, day of the week, moon phases, month and appropriate zodiac sign ... as well as the tide in Amsterdam! And then there's the ubiquitous restaurant offering traditional Cape fare – the buffet here is the gossip of the winelands. Equally whispered about are the picnic lunches on lawns shaded by pine trees, whose focal point is a lily pond beside the latticework of a pretty Victorian gazebo. Oh ... wine tasting in the *taphuis* or under the oaks is also pretty fine!

▛ Top Tip

Purr with the cuddly young cheetahs found in enclosures on Spier's estate. Part of a controlled breeding programme, all funds go towards the Cheetah Conservation Fund.

SPIER ▲

There are no flies on this impressive complex that sprawls alongside the Eerste River: a wine farm, three restaurants, a wine shop and a delicatessen / farm stall adjoining pretty picnic grounds lying around a lake and decorated with canvas umbrellas and wooden benches. That's not all: an impressive open-air theatre has hosted an extensive repertoire of dance, theatre, jazz, classical concerts ... and even opera. You can't miss it – it's presided over by gilded life-size statues of the Muses. Classical Greece comes to Wine Country. On matters of the stomach,

The Hottentots Holland mountain range has fantastic fynbos diversity, is popular with hikers and offers magnificent views from its numerous trails.

View of homestead and trees at Vergelegen Wine Estate.

SOMERSET WEST

In front of Vergelegen's manor house stand five old camphor trees that were planted in 1700 by the Cape governor, Willem Adriaan van der Stel. This large town lies to the south of the Stellenbosch winelands and has False Bay as one neighbour and the rugged Hottentots Holland mountains – the route to the Overberg – as another. The pride of the area is the Vergelegen Wine Estate ... and its ochre-walled, thatched and gabled manor home once belonged to a different Van der Stel. Willem Adriaan's claim to fame? He was demoted by the Dutch East India Co. for unfettered spending and incompetence, and deftly removed from his post.

DRINKING OF THE VINE

Vergelegen has a unique, gravity-fed underground cellar – grapes are fed into destalking, crushing and steel maturation tanks from above ground, thus maximising the effects of gravity and minimising bruising of the grapes. The theory goes that gentler grape handling produces smoother, rounder wines ... so the tree-huggers may well have a point, after all! If it's tea you're after (not wine!), the flower-bedecked Lady Phillips Tea Garden will wrap you round its pretty little finger. The garden was named in honour of Lord and Lady Phillips, who lived here from 1917 to 1940.

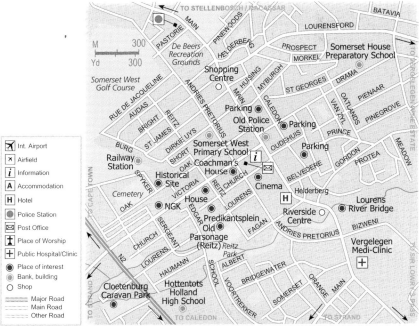

Monkey Town (close to Strand and Gordon's Bay) is a refuge and rehabilitation centre for primates. Visitors must walk through cages to look at the monkeys!

Casting a line into the ocean at dusk proves popular with locals and tourists.

STRAND

Strand ('beach' in Dutch and Afrikaans) is a modern town lying just south of Somerset West, on the furthest extent of False Bay's shores. From here swathes of white sand, like the broad blade of a scythe, curve all the way to Muizenberg, with the R310 running almost parallel to the coastline. The Strand promenade and restaurant jut out into the ocean, and beaches are packed in the holiday seasons (mental picture: sardines in a tin!).

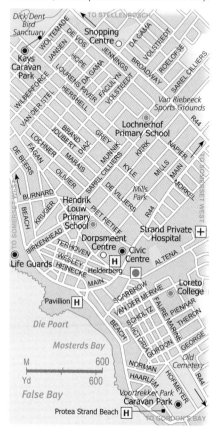

GORDON'S BAY ▶

Once a simple fishing harbour, Gordon's Bay has grown up. Now a very fine yacht club is flanked by swish holiday apartments and seaside homes, and the bay looks like some Mediterranean resort with the constant to-ing and fro-ing of glam yachts, motorboats and (not-so-glam) fishing vessels. If you're in luck and the shoals are running, you can charter a deep-sea boat to test your mettle with tunny and yellowtail. Bikini Beach has been earmarked for sunworshipping (what did you think?), while Main Beach is marked by testosterone – it's the active watersports zone of coloured sails, shrieking laughter, spraying water and the racket of twin-horsepower engines.

Clarence Drive offers delightful views and secretive coves.

■ Top Tip

Clarence Drive (from Gordon's Bay) tightly snakes its way between the coastline and the stony Hottentots Holland slopes all the way to Pringle Bay, and almost within spitting distance of the heaving seas. Dare we say ... it rivals Chapman's Peak!

JONKERSHOEK AND HOTTENTOTS HOLLAND ▶

The rough and rugged mountains of Stellenbosch, Somerset West and Gordon's Bay allow hikers and nature lovers to dust off technology and big-city pressures. To the east of Stellenbosch, sandwiched between the town and Jonkershoek mountains lies the Jonkershoek valley. Part of the Jonkershoek State Forest, walkers can hike through dense wooded forests and swim in crystal streams running over pebbled riverbeds. Idyllic? There are high waterfalls, wildflowers in summer, and mountain birds to spot – including Black Eagle, Peregrine Falcon and Mountain Buzzard. If you're into trees, you can identify the highly protected hardwood species – yellowwood, stinkwood and ironwood – that are not quite fully depleted by the early settlers who loved their fine-grained timber (and which proved perfect for the finest Cape furniture).

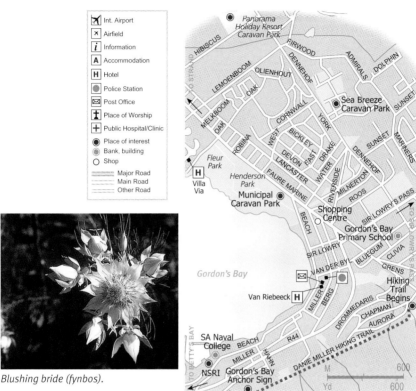

Legend:
- ✈ Int. Airport
- ✕ Airfield
- *i* Information
- Ⓐ Accommodation
- Ⓗ Hotel
- ⬤ Police Station
- ✉ Post Office
- ✝ Place of Worship
- ✚ Public Hospital/Clinic
- ⬤ Place of interest
- ⬤ Bank, building
- ◯ Shop
- Major Road
- Main Road
- Other Road

Blushing bride (fynbos).

Yet further to the east is the Hottentots Holland Nature Reserve covering an area of 400ha (988 acres) – challenging terrain for walkers who've progressed beyond baby steps and are ready for the real world. Cars have to stay behind, as this is serious hiking: backpacks with sleeping gear and food and cooking utensils. The Boland Trail runs through the reserve, a three-day, 41km (25-mile) route through fynbos, across stony hills and along goose-bump-chilly mountain pools. The trail has also been downsized into shorter, circular sections for those not quite ready to rough it under the stars for two nights.

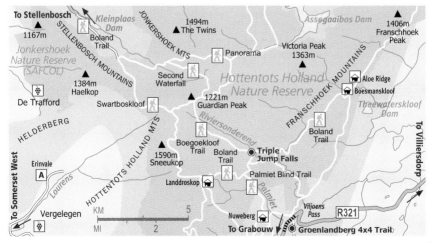

35

The Dutch settlers coined the name Swartland ('black land'), most likely because renosterbush, a local shrub, turns the veld dark in winter.

It's perhaps a combination of the cold upwelling of the Benguela Current (nourishing the dark kelp forests that sway lazily in the wind-blown, big-waved seas) and the stark and rocky coastal landscapes that give the West Coast its wild air. This, coupled with the barren, almost desert-like conditions inland where rain is scarce and summers are ferocious, creates a sometimes-forbidding picture. But that's not taking into account two major rivers: the Orange in the far north (on Namibia's border) and the Olifants, snaking from its mouth to the north of Lambert's Bay into Clanwilliam Dam and through Citrusdal. Both rivers have been harnessed extensively to irrigate citrus orchards, wheatfields and vineyards. As a bonus, at Clanwilliam the Olifants is backed by the craggy, contorted Cederberg mountains. The N7 highway forges a route straight up the West Coast, from Milnerton right up to the Namibian border: crossing the Swartland, it connects Malmesbury (centre for this region's wheat industry and proud home of the country's largest flour mills) with Citrusdal, Clanwilliam and Vanrhynsdorp's spectacular spring-flower displays.

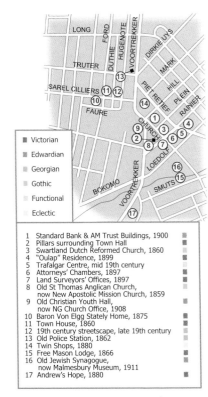

- Victorian
- Edwardian
- Georgian
- Gothic
- Functional
- Eclectic

1 Standard Bank & AM Trust Buildings, 1900
2 Pillars surrounding Town Hall
3 Swartland Dutch Reformed Church, 1860
4 "Oulap" Residence, 1899
5 Trafalgar Centre, mid 19th century
6 Attorneys' Chambers, 1897
7 Land Surveyors' Offices, 1897
8 Old St Thomas Anglican Church, now New Apostolic Mission Church, 1859
9 Old Christian Youth Hall, now NG Church Office, 1908
10 Baron Von Elgg Stately Home, 1875
11 Town House, 1860
12 19th century streetscape, late 19th century
13 Old Police Station, 1862
14 Twin Shops, 1880
15 Free Mason Lodge, 1866
16 Old Jewish Synagogue, now Malmesbury Museum, 1911
17 Andrew's Hope, 1880

A scenic view of Malmesbury's Swartland.

MALMESBURY HISTORIC WALK ▲
The local tourist bureau's 'historic route' brochure will guide you through the wide range of architectural styles gracing the town center. There's Gothic Revival style, Georgian, Edwardian, Victorian and even the eclectic twin shops in Piet Retief Street (1880).

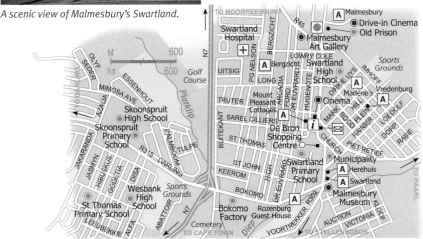

Die Strandloper serves delicious fresh-baked potbrood *and seafood in an unpretentious setting: beach sand and reed shelters in a protected cove.*

LANGEBAAN ▼

The lagoon is what makes people come back for more to the sleepy town of Langebaan. Part of the West Coast National Park and an important wetland for birdlife, the lagoon's 16km (10-mile) expanse turns a delicate shade of pink at certain times of the year as masses of crimson-winged flamingos descend on its waters. Hartlaub's Gulls, ibis, herons, and curlews also get a look-in, while Cape Cormorants hang out their wings to dry and White Pelicans try hard not to look like clowns. Human action comes in Smartie-pack hues – Hobie cats, wind-surfers and para-sailers: name them, they're here.

Pelicans on Langebaan lagoon.

✈	Int. Airport
✕	Airfield
𝑖	Information
A	Accommodation
H	Hotel
●	Police Station
✉	Post Office
✝	Place of Worship
✛	Public Hospital/Clinic
●	Place of interest
◉	Bank, building
○	Shop
▭	Major Road
▭	Main Road

THE FLOWER ROUTE ▲

Every year between August and October, Spring puts on her prettiest bloom-bedecked frock. The official flower route covers vast distances, from the Tienie Versveld Reserve in Darling to the Orange River in the north, and can take up to three days to cover fully. The arid, stony, scrubby Namaqualand region has different climatic zones, with flower species (4000 at the last count) ranging from neon daisies, gazanias and mesembryanthemums, to hardy fleshy succulents to geophytes (bulbs, corms and tubers) like irises and bulbinellas. Visitors often need travel no further than the Postberg Nature Reserve on Langebaan Lagoon – an hour's drive – to enjoy a mesmerising magic-carpet ride.

Top Tip

Flowers open with the sun, so cloudy days are no good for viewing. Blooms are best between 11:00 and 16:00; ensure that you drive facing the opened petals, and with the sun behind you.

Flowers in full bloom down the West Coast.

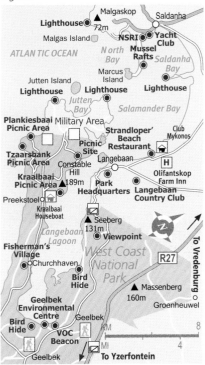

If you can chip and putt with the best, the Vredenburg golf course is making waves in West Coast golfing circles.

Locals from Paternoster in front of their home.

VREDENBURG & JACOBSBAAI

All roads lead to Vredenburg ... well, along the coast north of Saldanha, anyway. From here, the west-coast play-zones are all accessible: Jacobsbaai (Jacob's Bay, to those who can't get their tongue around the 'translation'), Paternoster, St Helena and Velddrif. Jacobsbaai is a beautiful, isolated spot of rocky peninsulas and sandy bays, focusing – naturally – on matters of the sea: scuba diving (in crayfish season), angling for linefish, collecting black mussels off the rocks, and dolphin and whale watching (between July and December). If this is *waaaay* too civilised for you, then rather hit the 17km (10,5-mile) easy-walking hiking trail from Swartriet, just north of Jacobsbaai, to Tietiesbaai. It crosses dune veld, fynbos and rocky coastal terrain; there are no trail facilities and a permit is required from the West Coast Council.

PATERNOSTER, ST HELENA

For a peek at how the fisherfolk live, Paternoster's village of traditional low-slung, small windowed, thatched fishermen's cottages will give you an idea. How did this village get its name? The story goes that when 17th-century Portuguese sailors were shipwrecked here, they recited the Paternoster (Lord's Prayer) to give thanks for their survival. Around the promontory to the north, St Helena Bay is another fishing village perched at the edge of a pretty bay. Some secret recipe of stark rocky coastline and frigid west-coast temperatures appears to have concocted a particularly turquoise hue in the waters of this coast. The coldness also nurtures healthy crayfish (Cape lobster), and scuba divers descend upon both villages in crayfishing season.

Top Tip

Trails in the Rocher Pan Nature Reserve will expand your nature-bent horizons to activities like fabulous birdwatching, spring flower-gazing, and southern right whale-spying.

Local men and children on their boat.

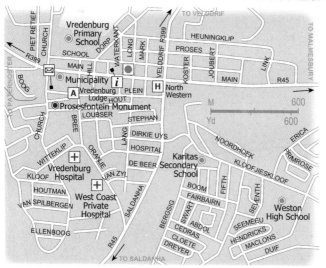

✈	Int. Airport
✕	Airfield
i	Information
A	Accommodation
H	Hotel
●	Police Station
✉	Post Office
✝	Place of Worship
●	Place of interest
●	Bank, building
○	Shop
	Major Road
	Main Road
	Other Road

Dwarskersbos is named after the humble candle bush (kersbosse), Velddrif after a 'drift' in the 'veld', and nearby Laaiplek stands for "loading place".

VELDDRIF

Velddrif has the advantage of two worlds: cold blue-green seas and the Berg rivermouth. Line-fishing, crayfishing, mussel-catching and sea-based watersports on the one hand, with birdwatching, canoeing, row-boating on the Berg on the other. Velddrif's world has also been enlivened by the development of an upscale holiday resort along its shores, attracting hordes of holidaymakers, come to let their hair down and play.

DWARSKERSBOS

A popular holiday resort, Dwarskersbos lies a quick drive north of Laaiplek and in the middle of the St Helena Bay basin. It boasts a brilliant, sandy beach that stretches as far as the eye can see. Back in '69 the town was wracked by a tidal wave that tore through the dune and swamped a number of houses. Whales can be spotted offshore, and the area has grown in popularity amongst anglers and watersports enthusiasts.

Top Tip

Enjoy bird-watching at Rocher Pan Nature Reserve, water sports at Port Owen Marina, local art at the West Coast Art Gallery, and the taste of the local West Coast delicacy, 'bokkom' (a salt fish).

Top: *Close-up of fishing boat.*
Above: *Wooden Jetty on Berg River at Velddrif.*

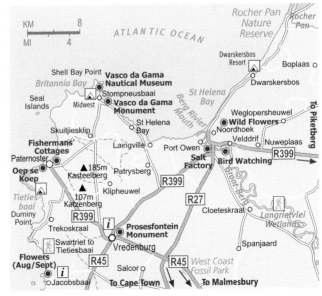

*The Snow Protea (*Protea cryophila*) – meaning 'fond of the cold'! – grows on Sneeuberg, the Cederberg's highest peak at 1028m (3372ft).*

The Maltese Cross has been crumbling for centuries – its upper section is made up of stronger Table Mountain sandstone.

CLANWILLIAM ▼

Another spot on the map whose body of water is more famous than the town: the 18km (11-mile) stretch of lake at the foot of the gnarled, weather-eroded Cederberg mountain range is mini-heaven for boaters and water-skiers. In summer they emerge soon after sunrise from holiday cabins, or the idyllically placed campsite nudging the water's edge, to glide across the dam's mirror-smooth surfaces before the winds stir. The dam, fed by the Olifants River, irrigates the surrounding farmlands and water can often be seen bursting through its sluice gates. The Cederberg mountains and surrounding area are named after the Clanwilliam cedar, which is today a protected species in the Cederberg Wilderness Area.

CEDERBERG HIKING ▶

The Cederberg range is part of the Cape Folded Mountains, its ingredients being sandstone, shale and quartzite, each being open to erosion to varying degrees. The result – powerful biting winds, dissolving rain and abrasion have nimbly and artfully sculpted a moonscape peopled by rocky gargoyles and goblins. No wonder walkers and overnight backpackers can't keep away from this place of bizarre and otherworldly 'creatures'. The 20m-high (65ft) Maltese Cross is a day-hike from Dwarsrivier, the impressive stone Wolfberg Arch (30m / 98ft) is less than a half-day away, and the Wolfberg Cracks are closer still, although it takes some squeezing, slithering and pushing from the rear to get there. Not for the half-hearted! Views from all the sites are quite stupendous. The monoliths of Tafelberg and Sneeuberg (2028m / 6654ft) can also be climbed.

TO DORINGBOS

GRAAFWATER

TO N7 / MALMESBURY / VANRHYNSDORP

R364

Blommenberg [A]

AUGSBURG

Saint Du Barry Country Lodge

Magistrates' Court

Municipal Offices

Supermarket

VOORTREKKER

MAIN

VISSER

[A] The Rectory Guest House

NORTIER

ARNOLD

LEIPOLDT

ROBERSON

MARKET

[i]

[H] Clanwilliam Museum

REENBLOM

HOSPITAL

Strassberger's

Clanwilliam Hospital

JAKARANDA

PARK

WOLTJIES

LOVE

M 300
Yd 300

HOSPITAL

WABOOM

Strassberger Shoe Factory

ORANGE

PROTEA

BUITENKANT

DENNE

Clanwilliam Dam Resort

[A]

OLD CAPE ROAD

SIPRES AVE

EIKE

GOUSBLOM AVE

SUIKERBOS AVE

BLOEKOM AVE

SONNEBLOM

Clanwilliam Dam

TO CITRUSDAL

✈	Int. Airport
✕	Airfield
i	Information
A	Accommodation
H	Hotel
●	Police Station
✉	Post Office
♁	Place of Worship
✚	Public Hospital/Clinic
◉	Place of interest
◉	Bank, building
○	Shop
	Major Road
	Main Road
	Other Road

Don't miss out on the San paintings (permits required) in their natural setting of surreal landscapes with names like Amphitheatre and Stadsaal ('city hall') caves; the spirit of such places is awesome.

Top Tip

Over countless centuries wind and water carved the Cederberg into a fairytale landscape: pinnacles, arches and bold fissures now decorate the landscape.

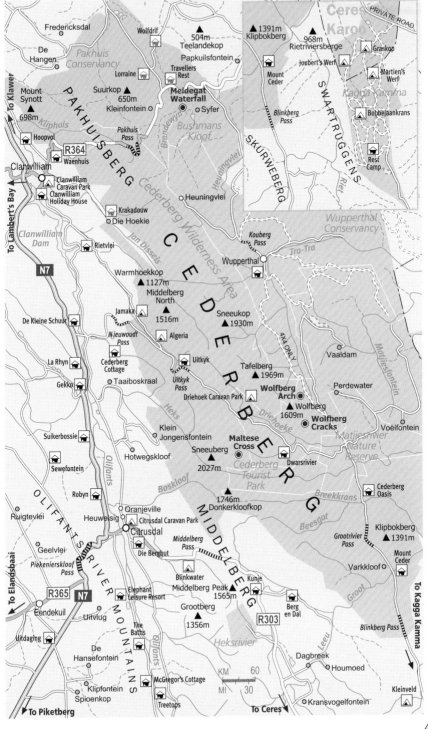

Spyhopping? Lobtailing? No, it's not Inspector Clouseau: it's the Southern Rights! Take the one-hour boat-trip (August to October) to find these whales.

Lambert's Bay

Lambert's Bay La

LAMBERT'S BAY

Two hours north of St Helena, Bird Island is what makes Lambert's Bay somewhat different. Accessed via a breakwater-cum-harbour wall, you'll smell the guano before you get to see the birds on their island breeding ground. Massed in their thousands are African (Jackass) Penguins, cormorants and Cape Gannets – fairest of them all with their airbrushed faces (could teach us women a thing or two about makeup ...). You can watch the birds' behaviour incognito from a viewing tower.

ELAND'S BAY

This coastline is an extension of the rocky, turquoise-dyed, crayfish-creviced West Coast. Eland's Bay, for one, is – you guessed it – mobbed by divers and their extended families in crayfish season, when the long arm of the law is lifted from December to April. Permits are your ticket to that tender, succulent, sweet-meat (brush with garlic and lemon butter, mmmm ...). A permit from any post office allows daily catches of four per person. On dry land, the terrain makes great offroad territory, and tourist information will supply you with a map of the best 4x4 trails.

Scenic view of gannets on Bird Island.

Top Tip

The Sandveld Museum in Lambert's Bay boasts unusual items, such as an old horse mill, a ginger jar (dated 1652, when Van Riebeeck landed), and a 300-year-old Bible written in High Dutch.

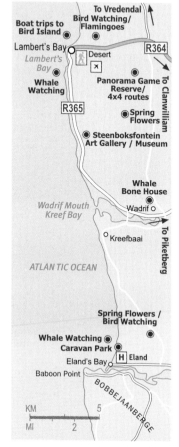

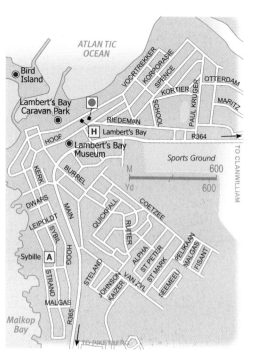

44

Vanrhynsdorp's attractions include the Latsky Radio Museum, Anglo-Boer war memorials and an old jail (1895) that now serves up crafts and coffee.

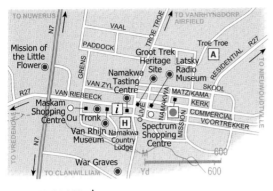

Hand prints on cave wall at Gifberg.

VANRHYNSDORP ▲

This town lies to the west of the Bokkeveld mountain range and is itself at the foot of the Matzikama mountains, settled in the pebble-strewn terrain of the *knersvlakte* – translating literally as 'gnashing plains'. Can't imagine it's too pleasant in baking mid-summer. Part of the Namaqualand flower route, Vanrhynsdorp's flower displays are mainly succulent *vygies* and Ursinia daisies. In the town itself, at the end of Voortrekker Street, visitors will find the country's biggest succulent garden and nursery, interesting for its rather outlandish plant forms, while further out is the Matzikama Eco Park. Southeast of Vanrhynsdorp is the Gifberg Pass, *gif* meaning 'poison' and referring to a poison-leafed bush that's scattered over the slopes. The pass also hides some great examples of San rock art. Views from here take in neatly clipped rows of vines, fields of wheat and rooibos tea of the Olifants River valley.

VREDENDAL ▶

Settled along the Lower Olifants River – and the centre of the Olifants irrigation scheme – Vredendal is a major agricultural hub. The town also links travellers with the beaches of the West Coast holiday resorts and is the gateway to Namaqualand and its Pandora's box of blooms. If you arrive at drinking time and you're ready to sup a little wine, Spruitdrift and Vredendal cellars will open their wine-tasting doors. Just hold your breath … it's still a fledgling wine industry here in the hot, dry Olifants River.

▌Top Tip

Vanrhynsdorp claims to offer the world's only succulent hiking trail, as well as some engrossing waterfalls. Star-gazing at night is also hugely rewarding away from big-city lights!

✈	Int. Airport
✕	Airfield
i	Information
A	Accommodation
H	Hotel
●	Police Station
✉	Post Office
♱	Place of Worship
✚	Public Hospital/Clinic
●	Place of interest
●	Bank, building
○	Shop
▬▬	Major Road
═══	Main Road
-----	Other Road

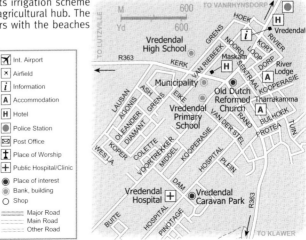

Witblits ('white lightning') is a lethal brandy-type potion, often distilled from peaches or grapes; its kick seems to do justice to its dramatic name.

BREEDE RIVER VALLEY & OVERBERG

South Africa's forebears definitely weren't kidding when they gave the Overberg its name. The entire region is one of soaring rock walls and chiselled passes – unless you've eased your way to the coastline. And don't be fooled here, either. Wild stormy seas and a deceptively rocky shoreline have seen the demise of a myriad of ships, furnishing Bredasdorp's quirky Shipwreck Museum with quite a collection of artefacts. But there is a gentler side to these seas – dolphins and whales. The most-spotted of the numerous dolphin species are the bottlenose, common and Heaviside's. Even more commonly spotted in-season (July to November) is the southern right whale. Of the world population (between 4000 and 6000) living in the icy sub-Antarctic seas, a great number of these southern rights migrate northward annually. Their gestation period lasts 12 months, they leave their breeding grounds from around June to calve and mate in the warmer, more protected South African coves and bays, often covering distances of up to 2600km (1615 miles) each year.

The wreck of the Oriental Pioneer (at a spot locals call Die Skip – the ship) is one of many to succumb along the coast near Agulhas, aka the "Graveyard of Ships".

WORCESTER ▼

Worcester is the biggest centre in the Breede River valley, owing to its industries of fruit, table grapes and winemaking, but the town's appeal lies elsewhere. You can make a splash on the Breede with countless watersport and outdoor activities to choose from, or get stuck into 4x4 trails in the Hex River's mountain territory. Or take it easy and sidle up to some succulents – the largest collection in Africa can be found at the Karoo National Botanic Garden. Ranked by the International Succulent Organisation as among the most

The Hex River Valley near Worcester.

authentic in the world, you can measure up to a *half-mens*tree ('half-human' – go check it out and you'll see why), size up the quiver trees (the San used its hollow bark branches as quivers for their arrows) or stare at the truly prehistoric welwitschias (which can live for thousands of years).

✈	Int. Airport
✈	Airfield
i	Information
A	Accommodation
H	Hotel
●	Police Station
✉	Post Office
†	Place of Worship
✚	Public Hospital/Clinic
◉	Place of interest
◉	Bank, building
○	Shop
===	Major Road
---	Main Road
···	Other Road

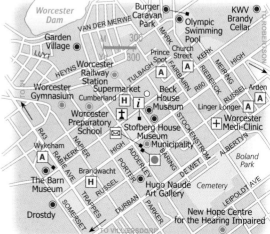

The Huguenot Tunnel has lopped 11km (7 miles) off the winding Du Toit's Kloof Pass, but the Paarl and Berg River Valley views are still great!

einplasie Robertson Kleinplasie Ro

ROBERTSON ▶

While Worcester hasn't quite made it in the wine stakes, Robertson comes out with flying colours. Its hot, sunny slopes tempered with plentiful irrigation have produced some powerful, flavour-packed white wines that flaunt themselves with a punch on the nose. Many of Robertson's cellars are award-winners, and you simply can't go wrong by visiting any of these: Bon Courage, De Wetshof, Springfield, Zandvliet or Graham Beck – the latter has an unusual, ultramodern, landscape-blending cellar called Madeba. Not Madiba, our much-loved proponent of peace. Beck's cellar means 'place of running water'.

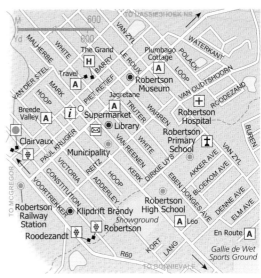

among others, tobacco-twisting, candlemaking, raisin-making and witblits-distilling. Water is drawn from a well using donkey-power and flour is ground by a horse-drawn mill. Naturally, an adjacent country market sells jams, homemade preserves, honey and cheeses. A taproom and restaurant will nourish hungry visitors and slake the deep thirst that sightseeing brings on.

Wine-tasting room, Graham Beck cellar.

KLEINPLASIE ▶

If you're keen to know how people managed before the days of mechanisation, electrification and technology, make a turn at the Kleinplasie Living Open Air Museum. A re-creation of the life lived by Dutch pioneers between 1690 and 1900, there are replicas of a labourer's cottage, a shepherd's hut and a coach house; activities practised daily are represented by a butchery, smithy, dairy and water mill. Year-round activities demonstrate,

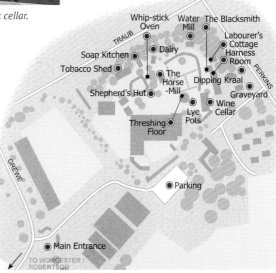

47

During harvest-time, towns along the Fruit Route invite visitors to indulge in fruit-picking – cherries, apricots, peaches, apples, pears and grapes.

Ceres Tulbagh Ceres Tulbagh

Woman carrying renosterveld near Ceres.

CERES ▼

Ceres nestles in a mountain-fringed basin simply bristling with fruit orchards. Name it and it's likely to feature – apple, pear, peach, nectarine, cherry, orange (even potatoes!). No surprise, then, that the town is named after the Greek goddess of agriculture (or the Roman corn goddess – depending on which way you look at it!). The local fruit-packing plant is the largest in the Southern Hemisphere; if you're serious about your vitamin C, you can embark on a two-hour fruit route. In winter, skiers head for the towering snow-clad Hex River mountains. Michell's Pass to the southwest of Ceres offers jaw-dropping scenery in its precipitous sandstone cliffs and ravines.

TULBAGH ▲

Tulbagh is akin to a living museum, despite its well-recorded earthquake in 1969 – something rather rare in South Africa – which measured 6.3 on the Richter scale and killed 8 people. Beautiful historic houses vie for attention on both sides of Church Street – 32 of the 18th- and 19th-century Cape Dutch and Victorian homes lining its entire length have been declared national monuments. It took five years to meticulously restore the extensive damage caused, and today many house tearooms / restaurants, art galleries, guesthouses and museums cater for tourists. The (very tall) Witzenberg and Winterhoek mountains encircling Tulbagh are heavily sugar-frosted most winters, which also draws the crowds in this generally no-snow country.

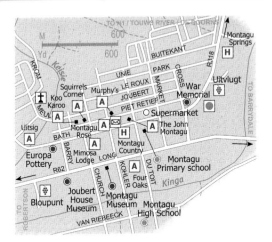

Montagu Pass: high rockfaces and a compelling geological history.

MONTAGU ▲

Yet again, history has left its legacy of historical architecture in this small town. Montagu's charm lies in its homes dating back to the 1850s, with 14 national monuments in Long Street alone. But the town is certainly better known for its natural thermal springs bubbling up at a constant 43˚C from deep within the earth. A hotel and resort has risen around the hot springs and does a humming trade. If the sulphur gets you hot under the collar, an entire series of trails along the northern edge of the Langeberg mountains for hikers, mountain bikers and 4x4 nutters, will get you excited.

SWELLENDAM ▶

At the foot of the Langeberg, gracious old Swellendam has the prettiest spot in the Overberg. The town grew around the Drostdy (magisterial centre), finished in 1746, and now crammed to the hilt with historic edifices – from

the Oefeningshuis in Voortrekker Street to the Drostdy (including the Old Jail) and Mayville museums on Swellengrebel. The Oefeningshuis was built as a church to give religious instruction – *godsdiensoefening* (read: 'educate') – to freed slaves. Note the plaster clockface on the gable with the real clock below it: the story goes, when the real hands matched the plaster clock, it was time to for everyone to assemble.

Top Tip

The Old Jail, part of the Drostdy Museum, has a wing of cells, plus a windowless 'black hole'. A trades yard behind the jail features a coppersmith, leather - worker, wagon-builder and wheelwright.

✈	Int. Airport
✈	Airfield
i	Information
A	Accommodation
H	Hotel
●	Police Station
✉	Post Office
✝	Place of Worship
✛	Public
●	Place of interest
◉	Bank, building
○	Shop
═══	Major Road
───	Main Road
───	Other Road

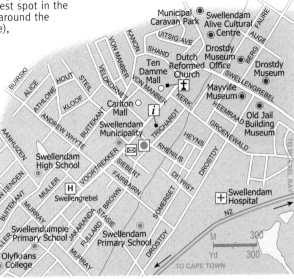

49

The rooms at the Post House are named after characters from books written by the classic children's author, Beatrix Potter.

GREYTON ▼

Encroached on by the tall Riviersonderend mountains, Greyton has been sought out by artists, craftspeople and small farmers, who live here in charming little dolls' houses with pitched tin roofs, painted shutters and iron lacework. Don't expect any va-va-voom here – only rest, peace and tranquility. Two guest houses – Greyton Lodge and The Post House, in similar Cape vernacular style – offer delectable dinners and great lodgings if you'd prefer not to have to roll home. A fynbos nature reserve bordering the town has several walking trails that snake into the Riviersonderend mountains.

have kept to simple Cape lines – whitewashed walls, little square windows, thatched roofs – and without the frills and furbelows.

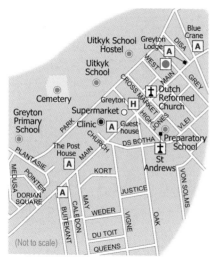

MCGREGOR ▶

Yet another of the country's perfectly preserved (like those old-fashioned pickles) Victorian villages. In an effort not to sound like a scratched gramophone record, the houses here, despite their Victorian influence,

GREYTON TO MCGREGOR HIKE (BOESMANSKLOOF TRAVERSE)

This 5-hour walking trail through a cleft in the Riviersonderend mountains can be tackled from either village: it's 14km (8,7 miles) from Die Galg, southwest of McGregor, or Main Street, Greyton. The views are great and you get to swim in the pools of the Oakes falls, 9km (5,6 miles) from Greyton. There are no huts; permits are necessary.

Old bicycle outside 'die smouswinkel'.

Since 1552, more than 150 ships have foundered on the southern Cape coast – that's one shipwreck for every kilometre of coastline!

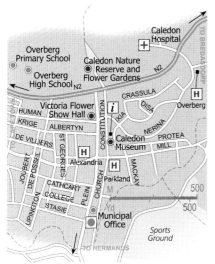

winds of this southern stretch of coast (earning the name 'graveyard of ships') have seen enough shipwrecks to make sure the museum is well-stocked with mini-treasures, artefacts – for example, a medicine chest from the *Clan McGregor* (1902) – and even blistered ship's figureheads. The museum, itself housed in the old rectory and church hall, is furnished as a 19th-century townhouse (with a marine flavour, of course).

Top Tip

Bredasdorp is the perfect base for exploring a number of nearby nature reserves: De Hoop, De Mond and Heuningberg Nature Reserve, the latter the beautiful and endemic red Bredasdorp lily.

CALEDON ▲

In the late Victorian era in the Overberg, Caledon was once the Southern Hemisphere's most la-di-dah spa. Today, the entertainment era has twirled its baton and transformed the hot mineral springs into a casino, hotel and spa complex. De Overberger Hotel has risen on the site of the old Victorian baths and is now the focus of the fit-'n-healthy, who stay that way with horse riding, tennis and golf. If you're a party-pooper, the Caledon Nature Reserve and Wildflower Garden might show you its 135 protea species. It has bridges and picnic spots, and a 10km (6-mile) trail takes you past the 'window' rock formation (no guessing how it got its name).

BREDASDORP ▶

Surrounded by barley fields and grazing sheep, Bredasdorp – other than its role as the centre of the wool industry – is the access route to Cape Agulhas and Arniston. Its one and only highlight is its Shipwreck Museum. The rocky reefs and gale-force

The Shipwreck museum in Bredasdorp.

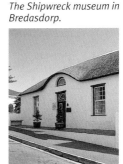

✈	Int. Airport
✖	Airfield
ℹ	Information
A	Accommodation
H	Hotel
●	Police Station
✉	Post Office
✝	Place of Worship
✚	Public Hospital/Clinic
●	Place of interest
◉	Bank, building
○	Shop
═══	Major Road
---	Main Road
····	Other Road

Haystacks, Caledon surrounds.

51

Hermanus is famed for its fresh and sparkling air, as well as offering some of the best land-based whale-watching spots in the world.

the mid-1800s. Its Harbour Museum contains fishing artefacts and bleached whalebones. From June to December (peaking during September and October) southern right whales come to calve in Walker Bay, drawing scores of tourists. Walker Bay also nurtures some very fine vines back on dry land and its wineries are creating a real stir.

Hermanus has risen to the ranks of upscale weekend and holiday resort so fast that it has overtaken itself. Massive development and the influx of playthings have made their mark. Sun-worshippers head for the beaches, aficionados of air and water hang-glide, para-glide, windsurf or paddleski, and pubs, restaurants and cafes buzz. Grotto Beach is the trendiest, but those who aren't here to 'be seen' go for long walks or horse-ride along Die Plaat, a silky 12km (8-mile) stretch from the lagoon to De Kelders. Hermanus focuses on the Old Harbour, whose restored fishing boats, lying hull-up, date back to

Top: *Old Harbour at Hermanus.*
Above: *Southern right whales.*

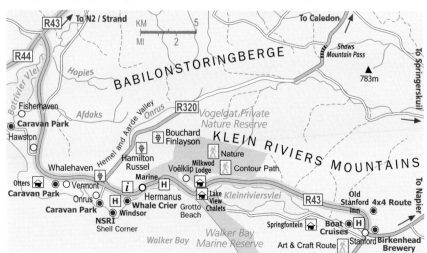

Migrating flocks arrive between September and April, while 12 of South Africa's 16 waterfowl species strut their stuff around these waters.

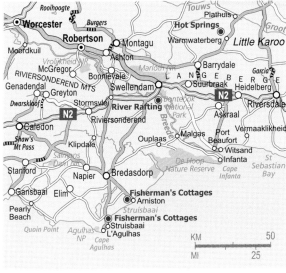

✈	Int. Airport
✕	Airfield
i	Information
A	Accommodation
H	Hotel
●	Police Station
✉	Post Office
✝	Place of Worship
✚	Public Hospital/Clinic
◉	Place of interest
◉	Bank, building
○	Shop
▦▦▦	Major Road
▬▬▬	Main Road
▭▭▭	Other Road

BREEDE RIVER VALLEY ▲

The Breede River has an abundance of activities: fruit routes, a wine route on canoe, river rafting, speed-boating, boardsailing, even mountain biking and 4x4 trails. Its waters are swelled by tributaries such as the Hex, Riviersonderend and Kingna. The Breede rises in the Ceres basin, cutting a deep gorge through the barrier of mountains that is traversed by the Michell's Pass. Following the pass road, the river visits Worcester, Robertson, Bonnievale and Swellendam, emptying into the Indian Ocean at Witsand.

DE HOOP NATURE RESERVE ▼

Two words describe it: simply *magnifique*! The 50km (31 miles) shoreline of De Hoop is pristine, particularly the stretch presided over by 90m-high (295ft) sand dunes. A marine reserve extending 5km (3 miles) into the ocean draws swimmers and divers; a 14km (9 miles) lagoon pulls wannabe-ornithologists. A short circular drive to Tierhoek may reveal the striped Cape Zebra and small antelopes, while mountain bikers can enjoy various trails in the Potberg section of the reserve.

Stretch of beach in the De Hoop Nature reserve.

The Wilderness Lakes (a loop of sinuous waterways, lakes, a lagoon and estuary) offer bird-watching trails guaranteed to get you close to the tweeters.

GARDEN ROUTE & ROUTE 62

When the stretch of coast between Mossel Bay and the Storms River mouth was encountered by early 17th- and 18th-century travellers (who were busy plying the trade routes to the East on their lateen-sailed caravels), the thickly forested slopes had not yet been plundered by rapacious settlers. As a result, their notebooks and diaries were filled with effusive descriptions that – over the centuries – were honed to its present epithet: the Garden Route. French traveller François Le Vaillant recorded his impressions of this coast in 1780 in his diary as 'an enchanted abode'. Today, unfortunately, the remaining stands of indigenous hardwoods – ironwood, yellowwood and stinkwood – are not as pervasive, yet they still manage to make a pretty impressive sight. The entire coastline is fed by countless rivers, drenching rains, and mists sweeping in from the sea, keeping it enduringly moist, fertile and green. This is punctuated by wave-lapped beaches, river mouths, lagoons and lakes, making it the natural playground for outdoor types – walkers and hikers, cyclists and mountain bikers, canoeists and board-sailors.

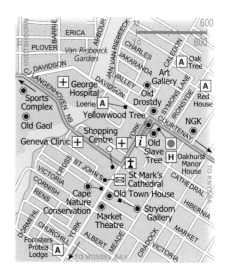

The Fancourt Country Club.

GEORGE

Lying as it does in the shadow of the Outeniqua mountains, it's not surprising that George's heritage smells of newly turned wood. Centre for the timber industry, its indigenous forests of stinkwood and yellowwood have set up more than a few factories. If you're proud of your golf swing, don't miss the luxury Fancourt Hotel and Country Club: gorgeous greens – the 27-hole course is designed by Gary Player – and for non-golfers, gooey kilo-shedding spa treatments to unveil the swan in you.

Top Tip

The 7-day, 108km (67-mile) Outeniqua hiking trail is popular but tough, over mountains, along a rocky coastline and through heaving forests. Book ahead!

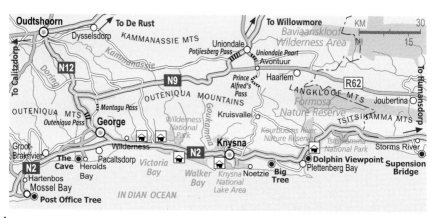

The lighthouse at Cape St Blaize is manned 24-hours-a-day ... one of only two such diligent warning beacons on the South African coast.

Mossel Bay Mossel Bay

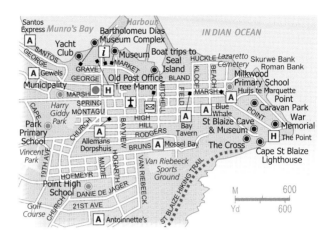

MOSSEL BAY ▲

This spot was first visited in 1488 by Portugese explorer Bartolomeu Dias, who encountered Strandlopers ('beach-wanderers'), a nomadic clan of the Khoi, living off mussels (after which the bay is known) and other yields of the coastline. Mossel Bay is the official start of the Garden Route, but it is more famous for its natural gas deposits, which are converted to oil at the controversial Mossgas development, eking billions our of state coffers. For the idiotically brave, shark cage-dives operate out of the town. Mossel Bay has built a reputation for serving up fantastic mussels, oysters, sole and even marlin.

DIAS MUSEUM ▼

This museum was established in 1988 to celebrate the 500th anniversary of Dias' historic landfall. His 25-ton wooden caravel was reconstructed in Portugal and sailed to Mossel Bay, arriving there in February 1988. The museum was specially modified to accommodate the vessel: an angled roof for the lateen masts and sails, with a sunken floor for its keel. Outside stands a milkwood tree from which a suspended shoe held letters left behind by seafarers. Today, a stone boot acts as a mailbox for visitors'

postcards, which are duly marked with a special stamp. Especially pretty are the jewel-bright stained-glass windows commemorating the early voyages of discovery. Even to non-history yobbos, the old maps, photographs and documents detailing early 15th-century explorations are of interest.

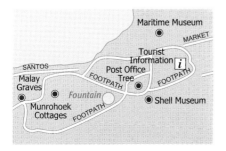

Top: *Dias museum interior.*
Above: *Cape St Blaize at the Point, Mossel Bay.*

55

North of Knysna, Noetzie's stone castles (some private homes, some bed-'n-breakfasts) line a stunning curve of beach are accessible via steep stairs.

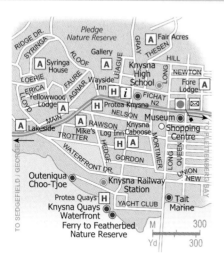

Choo-tjoe train crossing a bridge.

KNYSNA LAGOON
The serene 17km-long lagoon is guarded at its sea entrance by two sandstone cliffs, the Knysna Heads. If it's buzz you want, find it at the Knysna Quays Waterfront. Act cool on the terraces of Dry Dock or 34°South, both with great views onto waterways carrying yachts and boats chugging to and fro, where a nearby pedestrian bridge regularly lifts to accommodate passing masts into the marina. When it comes to the locals, Knysna equates to a constituency of Woodstock (leather sandals and tie-dye) and New Age (fairies and crystals).

OUTENIQUA CHOO-TJOE
Leaving from George at 08:10 and arriving in Knysna at 11:30, this narrow-gauge steam train slowly huffs and puffs around precipitous cliffs, crossing bridges, hooting its way over lakes and chugging through gum and pine forests. The leisurely trip takes three hours and culminates in a crossing of the 2km (1-mile) bridge that spans the Knysna Lagoon, before pulling into the station amid much noise and steam. The train leaves again at 12:55, arriving back in George at 16:10.

Top Tip
From Diepwalle Forest Station in the Kranshoek area, the Elephant Walk Nature Trail threads through towering indigenous trees, also passing the King Edward VII Big Tree (a yellowwood).

THE FRESHEST OYSTERS IN TOWN
Every year, in early July, this holiday spot (twice voted the best of the country's tourist towns) puts on her party pearls for the Knysna Oyster Festival. A bountiful supply of the freshest oysters, farmed in the Knysna lagoon, slip their cold slimy way down countless throats, chased by a squeeze of lemon and the fiery breath of Tabasco. Best done at the Knysna Oyster Co. on Thesen's Island – right next door to Knysna's very own locally brewed, richly flavoured draught ale at Mitchell's Brewery.

A castle at Noetzie.

✈	Int. Airport
✕	Airfield
i	Information
A	Accommodation
H	Hotel
●	Police Station
✉	Post Office
✝	Place of Worship
+	Public Hospital/Clinic
◉	Place of interest
◎	Bank, building
○	Shop
▬▬	Major Road
──	Main Road
═══	Other Road

Between Nature's Valley and the Storm's River mouth are two famed trails – Tsitsikamma and Otter – through rugged mountains and tangled forest.

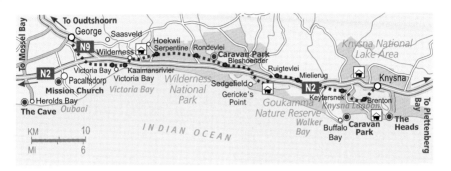

If the depth of your pockets rates you in the big bucks league, you'll spend your (local) holidays in this razzle-dazzle town. Perched prettily above a lagoon formed by the Keurbooms and Bitou rivers, 'Plett' (to those who frequent it) in summertime gives you good shopping, better eating, cappuccinos and cocktails, bronzed babes and oiled biceps. When this all gets too much for you, head out to the Robberg Peninsula, a nature and marine reserve where cliff-high walks and tightrope views onto secret-hideaway beaches and the boiling seas below will definitely clear your head. Schools of dolphins riding the waves are not uncommon, likewise whales, in season.

Top: *Dolphins playing in the surf.*
Above: *Sea-kayaker's on the beach.*

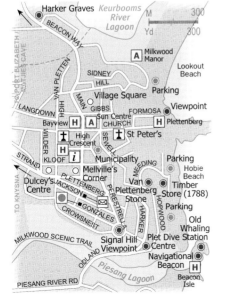

The camp in the Karoo National Park is highly civilized, with chalets in the Cape vernacular, a pool, restaurant and even a caravan park.

KLEIN KAROO
(LITTLE KAROO)

The Karoo (a vast, dry expanse of desert-like terrain) stretches across sections of the Western Cape and into the Northern Cape. It is divided into the Little and the Great Karoo, according to geological factors as well as topography, vegetation and climate. The name 'karoo' derives from the indigenous Khoi people's description, 'land of great thirst'. Far from devoid of life, the Karoo boasts the world's greatest and largest amount of succulents, with more than 9000 in the Beaufort West region. The scenery is flat, monotonous, and stretches to every horizon, but here and there outcrops bear evidence of typical Karoo shale and sandstone strata, layered like pancakes. At times the monotony of the landscape is also broken by dolerite formations where volcanic lava has thrust up through the earth, and over time been weathered into weird and wonderful shapes as the harder rock resisted the moulding and reshaping forces of wind and water. Some are highly distinctive, with names like the Three Sisters – three similarly shaped conical hills – north of Beaufort West. An enduring image of this slice of South African landscape is, here and there, a lone wind pump, like a sentinel in the crisp, eternally clear Karoo air.

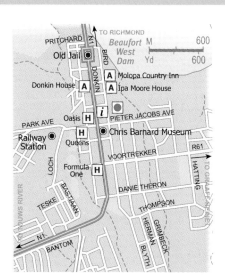

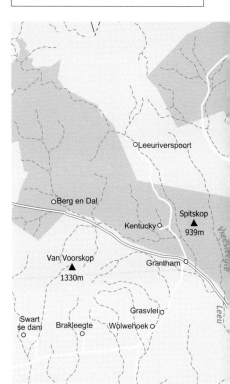

Still Life in Beaufort West.

Top Tip

The Karoo (Hottentot for 'dry thirstland') is a baking, arid and desolate region, and boasts an ancient history that offers up a plethora of fossils from its swamp days.

Symbol	Legend
✈	Int. Airport
✕	Airfield
i	Information
A	Accommodation
H	Hotel
●	Police Station
✉	Post Office
✝	Place of Worship
✛	Public Hospital/Clinic
●	Place of interest
◉	Bank, building
○	Shop
═══	Major Road
---	Main Road
····	Other Road

BEAUFORT WEST

The N1 – the Great North Road, connecting Cape Town with Johannesburg – bisects the Karoo. Beaufort West, the 'capital' of the Karoo region (or at least its largest town!) is located on the N1. The town has little to commend it, other than its role as a centre of civilisation in the flat, featureless middle of nowhere. Travellers can find a basic, clean place to stay overnight, fill their travel-weary tums, refuel their equally travel-weary vehicles, and then fill it with lots of treats to stave off boredom from the many hours spent on the road.

Accommodation in the Karoo National Park.

KAROO NATIONAL PARK

Just north of Beaufort West, the vast flat plains of the Karoo National Park are deceptive in the sweet green fodder they so obviously provide to kudu, hartebeest and springbok. Other wildlife has been re-introduced, 'big guns' such as black rhino, black wildebeest – 'gnu' is an apt name for a creature that looks like it's stepped out of *Jungle Book* – and Cape mountain zebra. Animal supreme is the gemsbok, with its rapier horns that seem to rip the air. The park has a 4x4 trail, and the Fossil (geology) and Bossie (vegetation) walking trails.

A Grey rhebok family, cleverly camouflaged on a rocky koppie (hill) in the Karoo National Park.

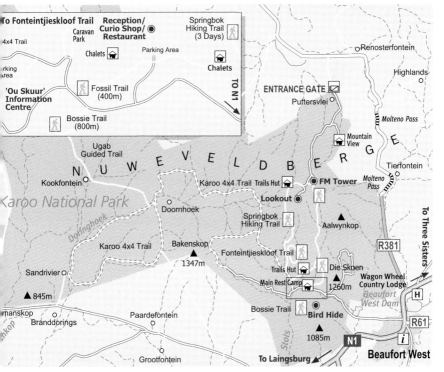

The iron lace that prettifies South Africa's Victorian homes is locally termed 'broekie' lace – a reminder of the delicate lace edgings of a lady's bloomers!

LAINGSBURG ▼

This town's dubious claim to fame is its brush with momentous floods in 1981. Laingsburg was laid out in 1881, along the banks of the Buffalo River, with a backdrop of rolling hills melding with the Klein Swartberg's sandstone mountain peaks. Ironically, its centenary year (which should have been one of celebration) was marked by uncharacteristically heavy rains, the result of which was that the river burst its banks, flooding the dry, sandy, unstable soils and causing major landslides. Much of the town was covered in river silts and muds. The Dutch Reformed Church was one original old building that remained unscathed.

MATJIESFONTEIN

A turn-of-the-century town centering on the 1900 Lord Milner Hotel, Matjiesfontein is in its entirety a national monument. It was all started by Scotsman James Logan in 1883, when he established a dining place alongside the railway line in an age when trains had no dining coaches. Over time, this expanded to become a hotel and today, Lord Milner's decorative iron-lace verandahs and white-painted square turrets are reminiscent of that elegant time. Despite the lattice-fringed post office nearby, Matjiesfontein is, essentially, a charming hotel complex planted in the middle of the Little Karoo.

The Lord Milner Hotel in Matjiesfontein: its guestbook is a name-droppers' delight!

Top Tip

Matjiesfontein boasts some interesting museums (the Transport Museum and the Marie Rawdon Museum), while a trip around town on the local London double-decker bus is a must.

A secret, stunning world unfolds alongside Seweweekspoort.

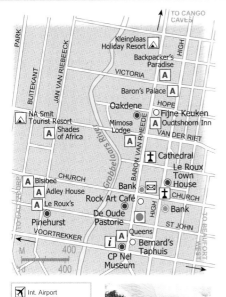

OUDTSHOORN

The country's ostrich-farming capital has earned its reputation, boasting grandiose sandstone mansions (aka 'feather' palaces), with dyed feathers, ostrich leather handbags, belts, shoes and painted eggs for sale. At the Cango Wildlife Ranch there are lion and cheetah to spy on (from a walkway), and crocodiles and alligators to snap their ugly teeth at you. If you're into 'magic-mushroom trips', visit the Cango Caves for the phantasmagorical limestone drip formations.

FOUR PASSES

Composed of rough-hewn rock and deep sky, the Four Passes has an amazing concentration of mountain landscapes, including the Swartberg, Langeberg and Outeniqua mountains. Pass builder Thomas Bain proved his mettle at the base of these rock barriers. Seweweekspoort rises to 2325m (7628ft), Schoemanspoort chisels through a 10km (6-mile) narrow chasm, Swartberg winds on for 24km (15 miles) and Meiringspoort bares its cliffs in contorted, burnt-orange folds.

Map Legend

- ✈ Int. Airport
- ✕ Airfield
- *i* Information
- A Accommodation
- H Hotel
- ● Police Station
- ⊠ Post Office
- ✝ Place of Worship
- ✚ Public Hospital/Clinic
- ● Place of interest
- ◉ Bank, building
- ○ Shop
- ═══ Major Road
- ─── Main Road
- ─── Other Road

Above: *Ride on an ostrich or cuddle the chicks.*
Left: *Multi-hued ostrich feathers are on offer.*

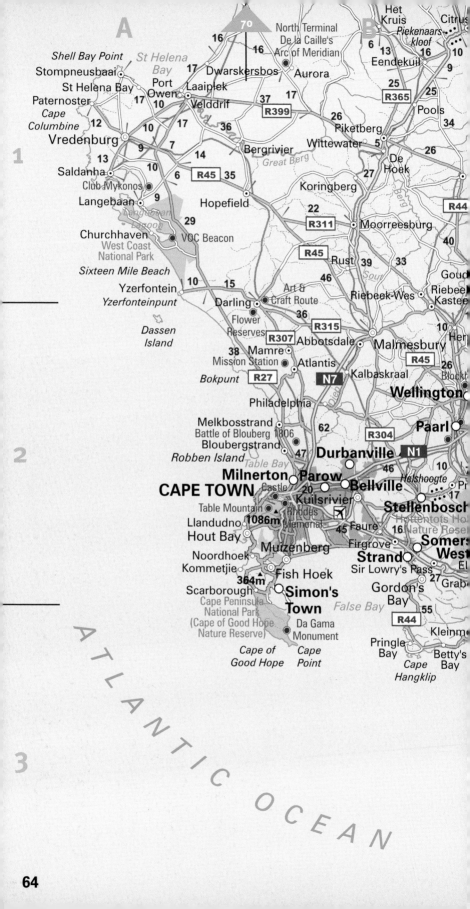

A

B

70

Shell Bay Point
St Helena Bay
Stompneusbaai
St Helena Bay
Paternoster
Cape Columbine
Vredenburg
Saldanha
Club Mykonos
Langebaan
Churchhaven
West Coast National Park
Sixteen Mile Beach
Yzerfontein
Yzerfonteinpunt

Het Kruis
Piekenaarskloof
Citrus

North Terminal
De la Caille's
Arc of Meridian
Aurora
Dwarskersbos
Laaiplek
Port Owen
Velddrif
Bergrivier
Great Berg
Hopefield
VOC Beacon

Eendekuil
Piketberg
Wittewater
De Hoek
Koringberg
Moorreesburg
Rust
Riebeek-Wes
Goud
Riebee
Kastee

Pools
34

R365
R399
R45
R311
R45
R315
R307
R27
R44
R45

16
16
6
13
16
10
9
17
17
25
25
26
25
37
17
26
5
26
36
12
10
17
22
40
13
9
7
14
27
39
33
10
6
35
46
10
9
10
29
36
10
15

Darling
Art & Craft Route
Flower Reserves
Mamre
Mission Station
Bokpunt
Atlantis
Abbotsdale
Malmesbury
Kalbaskraal
N7
Wellington
Philadelphia
Melkbosstrand
Battle of Blouberg 1806
Bloubergstrand
Robben Island
Table Bay
Milnerton
CAPE TOWN
Castle
Parow
Kuilsrivier
Durbanville
Bellville
Paarl
N1
Stellenbosch
Pr
17

38
62
47
20
46
45
16
55

R304
N1
R45
R44

Dassen
Island

Table Mountain
1086m
Rhodes Memorial
Llandudno
Hout Bay
Noordhoek
Kommetjie
Scarborough
364m
Fish Hoek
Simon's Town
Cape Peninsula National Park
(Cape of Good Hope Nature Reserve)
Cape of Good Hope
Cape Point
Da Gama Monument
Muizenberg
Faure
Firgrove
Strand
Sir Lowry's Pass
Gordon's Bay
False Bay
Grab
Pringle Bay
Kleinm
Betty's Bay
Cape Hangklip
Somers
West
Hottentots Ho
Nature Rese
Helshoogte
Blockt

ATLANTIC OCEAN

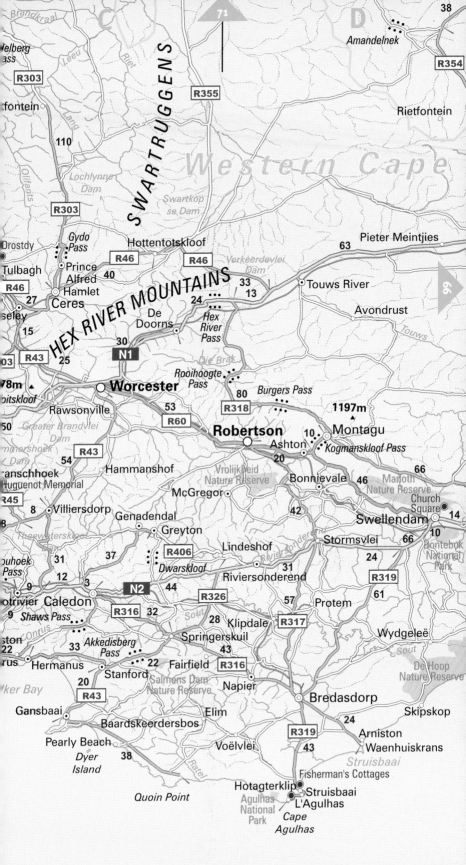

Brandkraal

C

71

D

38

Amandelnek

R354

Helberg ass

R303

fontein

Leeu

Riet

R355

Rietfontein

SWARTRUGGENS

110

Olifants

Lang

Lochlynne Dam

Western Cape

Swartkop se Dam

R303

Gydo Pass

Hottentotskloof

Drostdy

Prince Alfred Hamlet

R46

R46

Verkeerdevlei Dam

Pieter Meintjies

63

Tulbagh

40

33

Touws River

R46

Ceres

27

24

13

Avondrust

HEX RIVER MOUNTAINS

seley

15

De Doorns

Hex River Pass

30

Touws

R43

25

N1

Die Brak

03

78m

Rooihoogte Pass

Burgers Pass

Rawsonville

53

80

1197m

Montagu

Worcester

R318

10

R60

50

Greater Brandvlei Dam

Robertson

Ashton

Kogmanskloof Pass

R43

mmershoek Dam

54

Hammanshof

20

66

Vrolijkheid Nature Reserve

Bonnievale

46

Marloth Nature Reserve

anschhoek

Huguenot Memorial

McGregor

Church Square

R45

8

Villiersdorp

Genadendal

42

Swellendam

14

Greyton

Lindeshof

Stormsvlei

66

10

31

R406

24

Bontebok National Park

uhoek Pass

37

Dwarskloof

Riviersonderend

31

9

12

3

44

R326

57

R319

61

otrivier

Caledon

N2

Protem

Shaws Pass

R316

32

28

Klipdale

R317

Wydgeleë

9

Springerskuil

22

33

Akkedisberg Pass

43

Sout

ston

rus

22

Fairfield

R316

De Hoop Nature Reserve

Hermanus

Stanford

Salmons Dam Nature Reserve

Napier

20

R43

Elim

24

Skipskop

Gansbaai

Baardskeerdersbos

R319

Arniston

Pearly Beach

Dyer Island

38

Voëlvlei

43

Waenhuiskrans

Struisbaai

Quoin Point

Hotagterklip

Fisherman's Cottages

Struisbaai

Agulhas National Park

L'Agulhas

Cape Agulhas

65

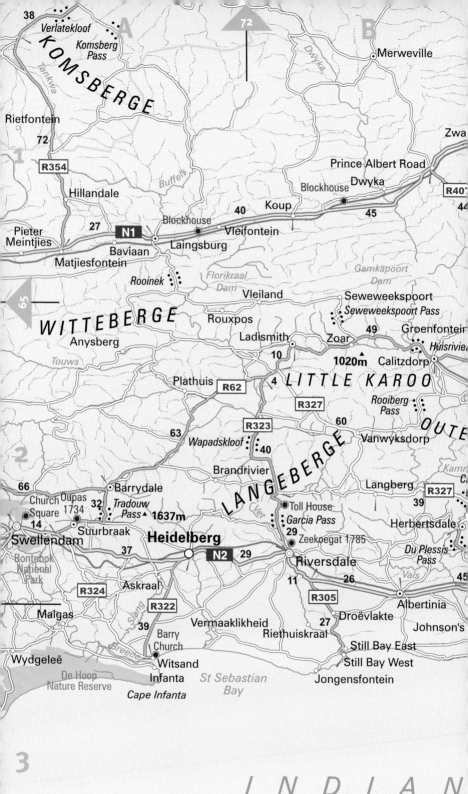

38

Verlatekloof

Komsberg
Pass

A

72

B

K O M S B E R G E

Merweville

Tankwa

Zwa

Rietfontein

72

Prince Albert Road

R354

Hillandale

Blockhouse

Dwyka

R40

Koup

40

Blockhouse

45

44

Florikraal
Dam

Gamkapoort
Dam

Pieter
Meintjies

27

N1

Blockhouse

Vleifontein

Laingsburg

Baviaan

Matjiesfontein

Rooinek

Vleiland

Seweweekspoort

Seweweekspoort Pass

65

W I T T E B E R G E

Rouxpos

Anysberg

Touws

Ladismith

Zoar

49

Groenfontei

Huisrivie

10

1020m

Calitzdorp

L I T T L E   K A R O O

4

Plathuis

R62

R327

OUTE

63

R323

Rooiberg
Pass

Wapadskloof

40

60

Vanwyksdorp

Kamr

Brandrivier

L A N G E B E R G E

Langberg

R327

C.

66

Barrydale

Church Oupas
Square 1734

32

Toll House

Garcia Pass

Herbertsdale

14

Tradouw
Pass

1637m

29

Zeekoegat 1785

Du Plessis
Pass

Suurbraak

Heidelberg

N2

Riversdale

Swellendam

37

29

Bontebok
National
Park

R324

Askraal

11

26

45

R305

Albertinia

Malgas

R322

39

Vermaaklikheid

27

Droëvlakte

Johnson's

Barry
Church

Riethuiskraal

Still Bay East

Wydgeleë

Witsand

Still Bay West

De Hoop
Nature Reserve

Infanta

St Sebastian
Bay

Jongensfontein

Cape Infanta

3

I N D I A N

R61
R338
Kendre
A
74
B
N9
39
Aberdeen
Road
Kaapse Poortjie
96
35   Oatlands
R338
Jansenvil
Klipplaat
44
Swanepoelspoort :. Miller ▲1450m Mount
Steward   34
Perdepoort : :. GROOTRIVIERBERGE
1414m   18   Bar
Willowmore   29   57   26
39   R329   Steytlerville
67 BAVIAANSKLOOFBERGE
Ghwarriespoort ▲1627m GROOTWINTE
N9
Sandvlakte
Studtis Baviaanskloof Colekeplaas
Zaaimansdal Sipres
Bavjaanskloof Camb
Wilderness Area
Kouga
Haarlem 70
Misgund   R62   Louterwater Andriesk
▲1618m
palmiet   Joubertina
40   Diep
Grootrivier Bloukrans
Pass   Pass   Formosa Nature Reserve
The   Storms River   Kareedouw   33
Crags
Wittedrif   54 Tsitsikamma   33 Clarkson
National   Storms River Woodlands
N2   Park   Mouth   37   N2   Impo
Plettenberg   Dan
Bay   Slangri
Cape
Seal   Oyster B

3

I N D I A N

68

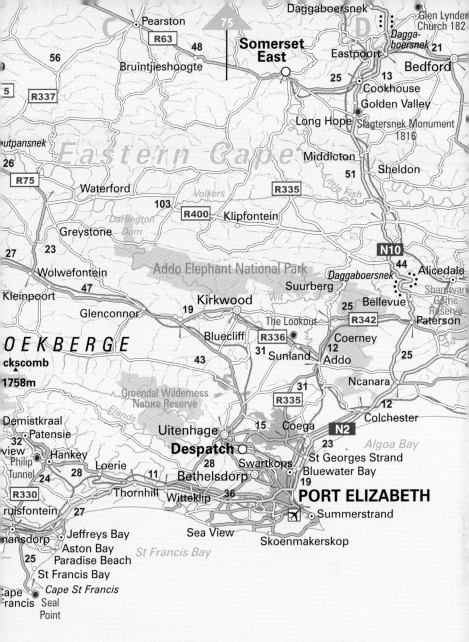

C · D

Pearston
R63
56
Bruintjieshoogte
48
75
Daggaboersnek
Somerset East
Eastpoort
25
13
Cookhouse
Golden Valley
Long Hope
Slagtersnek Monument 1816
Glen Lynder Church 182
Daggaboersnek 21
Bedford

R337
5
utpansnek
26
R75
Waterford
Greystone
Darlington Dam
Volkers
103
R400
Klipfontein
R335
Middleton
Sheldon
51
Little Fish

27
23
Wolwefontein
47
Kleinpoort
Glenconnor
OEKBERGE
ckscomb
1758m
19
Kirkwood
Addo Elephant National Park
Suurberg
Wit
The Lookout
R336
Bluecliff
43
31 Sunland
N10
44
Alicedale
Daggaboersnek
Bellevue
25
R342
Coerney
12 Addo
Paterson
Shamwari Game Reserve
25
Ncanara
31
R335
12
Colchester

Demistkraal
Patensie
32
view
Philip Tunnel
24
Hankey
28
Loerie
11
Thornhill
R330
ruisfontein
27
Groendal Wilderness Nature Reserve
Elands
Uitenhage
Despatch
28
Bethelsdorp
Witteklip
36
15
Coega
N2
23
St Georges Strand
Swartkops
Bluewater Bay
19
PORT ELIZABETH
Summerstrand
Sea View
Skoenmakerskop
Algoa Bay

nansdorp
25
Cape Francis
Jeffreys Bay
Aston Bay
Paradise Beach
St Francis Bay
Cape St Francis
Seal Point
St Francis Bay

Eastern Cape

OCEAN

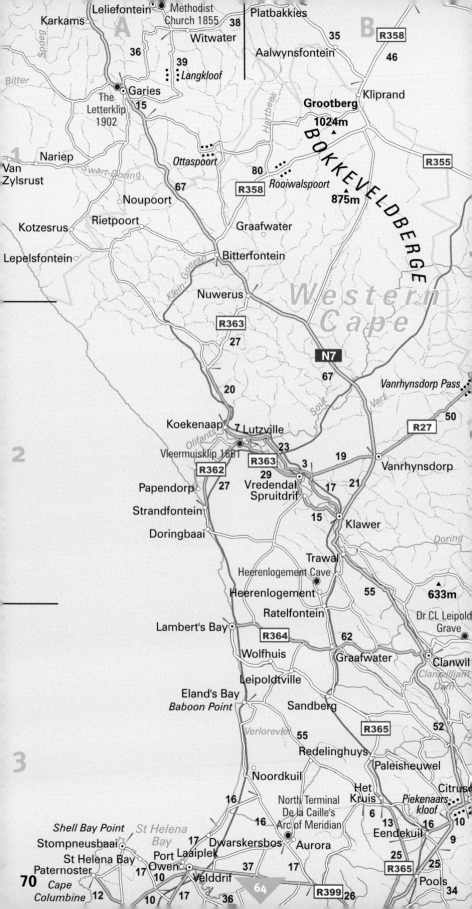

C   D

Commissioner's Salt Pan

Brandvlei

N o r t h e r n
C a p e

Brandboom   120   47   R353

R357   *Swartkolkvloer*

Tontelbos   Sakrivier

10   Loeriesfontein

Rietfontein   R27

R357   72

53   *Driekop Dam*   80   Kootjieskolk

R355

Brandkop   Hantam   97

euwoudtville   89

1673m

R27   34   Calvinia   R63

35   17

6

Keiskie se Poort

R354

Bloukrans Pass   64

otterkloof

Bloukrans   R355

63

Matjieskloof

Middelpos

R354

Doringbos

R364   Danielskuil

R364   Uitspankraal   Die Bos

Biedou

Biedouvvallei   Van Wyksvlei

81

146

euberg   *Tankwa*   Tankwa-Karoo
National Park

027m   Cederberg   Tweefontein   Bo-Wadrif

Oudebaaskraal Dam   38

Brandkraal   *Amandelnek*

Vis

Matjies

delberg   *Leeu*   *Riet*
ass

R303   R355   R354

65   71

fontein   Rietfontein

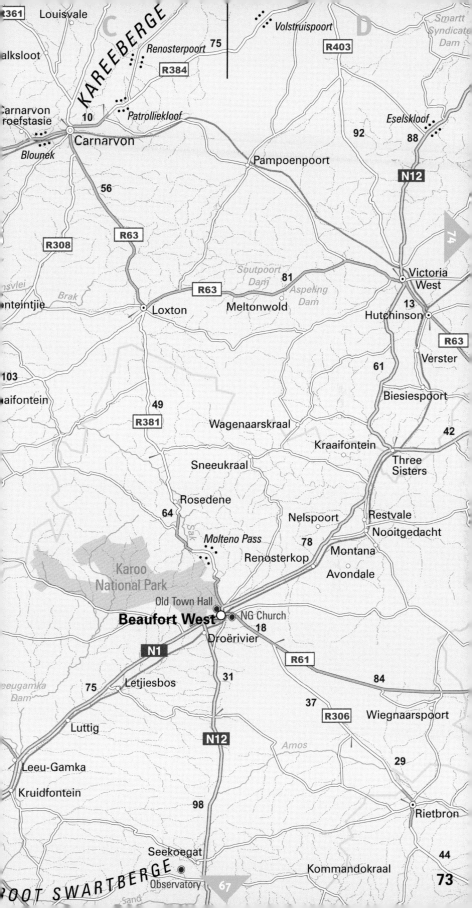

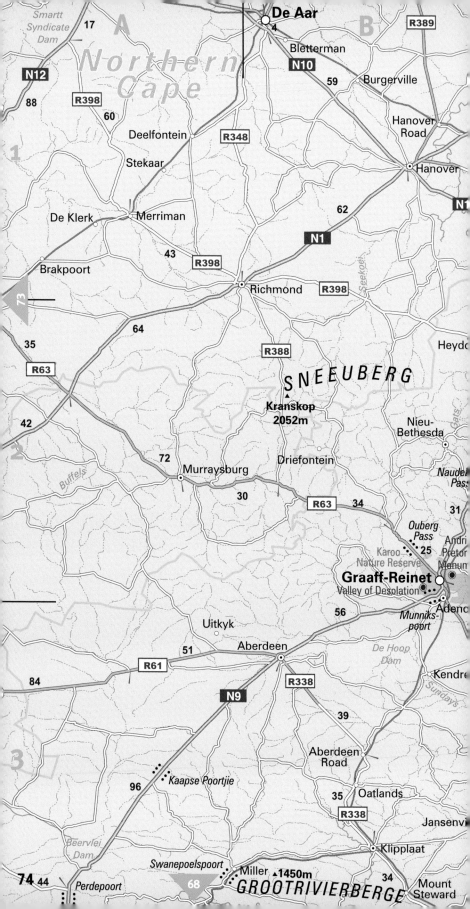

De Aar
4
Bletterman

Smartt
Syndicate
Dam

17

A

B

R389

N12

Northern
Cape

N10

59

Burgerville

88

R398

60

Hanover
Road

Deelfontein

R348

Stekaar

Hanover

N1

1

De Klerk

Merriman

62

N1

43

R398

N1

Brakpoort

Richmond

R398

73

64

35

R388

Heydo

R63

S N E E U B E R G

42

Kranskop
2052m

Nieu-
Bethesda

72

Murraysburg

Driefontein

Buffels

Naude
Pass

2

30

R63

34

31

Ouberg
Pass

Karoo
Nature Reserve

25

Andri
Pretor
Monum

Graaff-Reinet
Valley of Desolation

Uitkyk

56

Munniks-
poort

Adenc

Aberdeen

R61

51

De Hoop
Dam

Kendre

84

R338

Sundays

N9

39

3

Aberdeen
Road

96

Kaapse Poortjie

35

Oatlands

Jansenv

R338

Beervlei
Dam

Klipplaat

74 44

Swanepoelspoort

68

Miller ▲1450m

34

Perdepoort

GROOTRIVIERBERGE

Mount
Steward

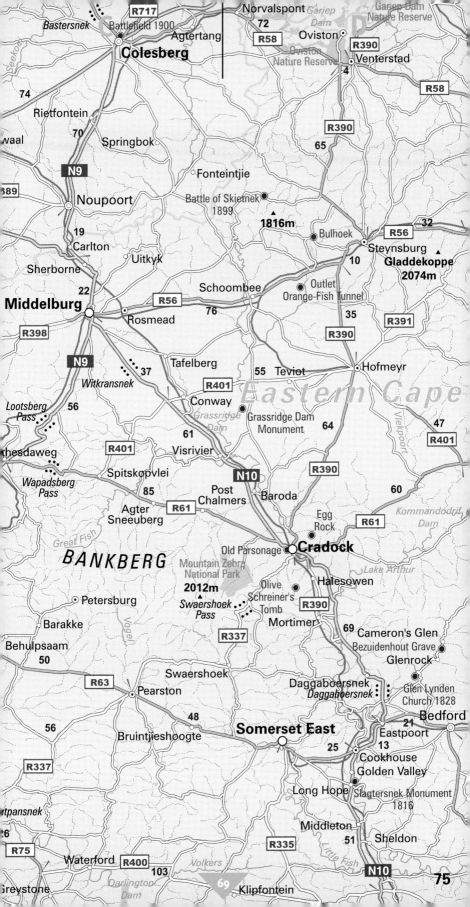

Bastersnek
Colesberg
Battlefield 1900
R717
Agtertang
Norvalspont
Gariep Dam
Nature Reserve
Gariep Dam
72
R58
Oviston
Oviston Nature Reserve
R390
Venterstad
4
R58
74
Rietfontein
70
Springbok
R390
65
N9
Fonteintjie
Battle of Skietnek 1899
1816m
Bulhoek
R56
32
Steynsburg
Gladdekoppe 2074m
Noupoort
389
19
Carlton
Sherborne
Uitkyk
Schoombee
10
waal
22
Middelburg
R56
Rosmead
76
Outlet
Orange-Fish Tunnel
35
R391
R398
R390
N9
37
Tafelberg
55
Teviot
Hofmeyr
Witkransnek
R401
Conway
Eastern Cape
64
47
R401
Lootsberg Pass
56
Grassridge Dam
Grassridge Dam Monument
Vlekpoort
61
Visrivier
thesdaweg
R401
Spitskopvlei
N10
60
Wapadsberg Pass
85
Baroda
R390
Kommandodrif Dam
Agter Sneeuberg
R61
Egg Rock
R61
Great Fish
BANKBERG
Post Chalmers
Old Parsonage
Cradock
Petersburg
Mountain Zebra National Park
2012m
Halesowen
Lake Arthur
Barakke
Swaershoek Pass
Olive Schreiner's Tomb
Mortimer
R390
69
Cameron's Glen
Bezuidenhout Grave
Glenrock
Behulpsaam
50
R337
Swaershoek
Daggaboersnek
Daggaboersnek
Glen Lynden Church 1828
R63
Pearston
Bedford
56
48
Bruintjieshoogte
Somerset East
25
21
Eastpoort
13
Cookhouse
Golden Valley
R337
Long Hope
Slagtersnek Monument 1816
tpansnek
Middleton
R75
51
Sheldon
Waterford
R400
103
R335
Volkers
N10
75
greystone
Darlington Dam
69
Klipfontein
Little Fish

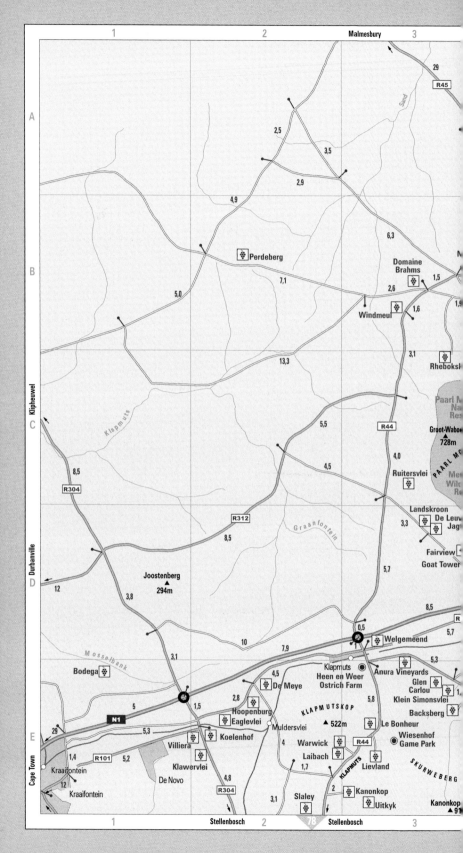

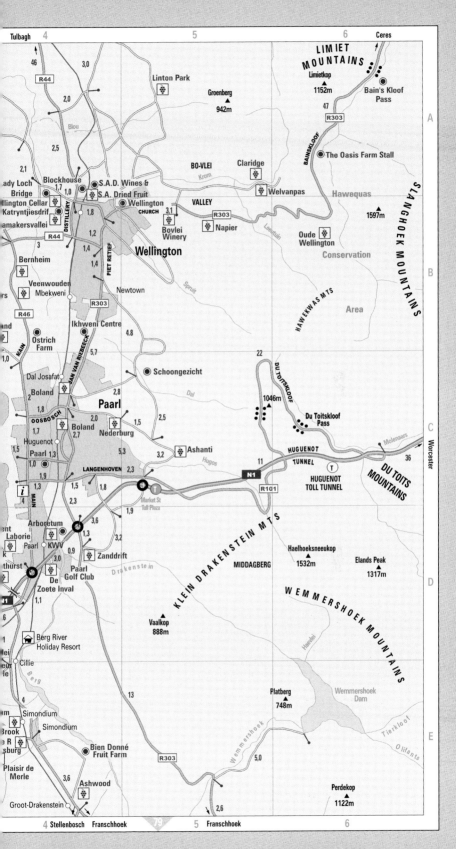

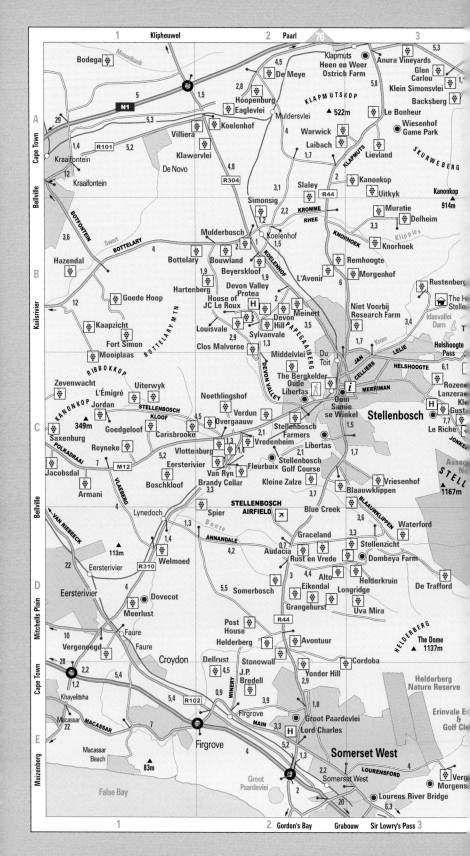

78   **Winelands**   **Scale 1 : 160 000**

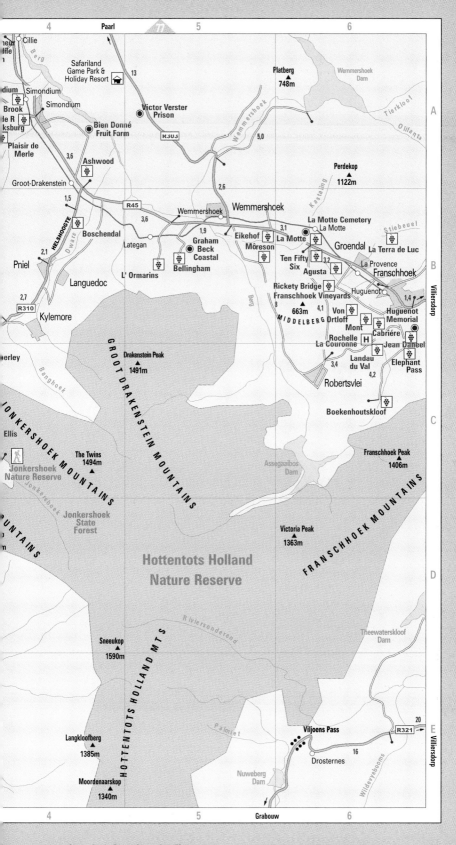

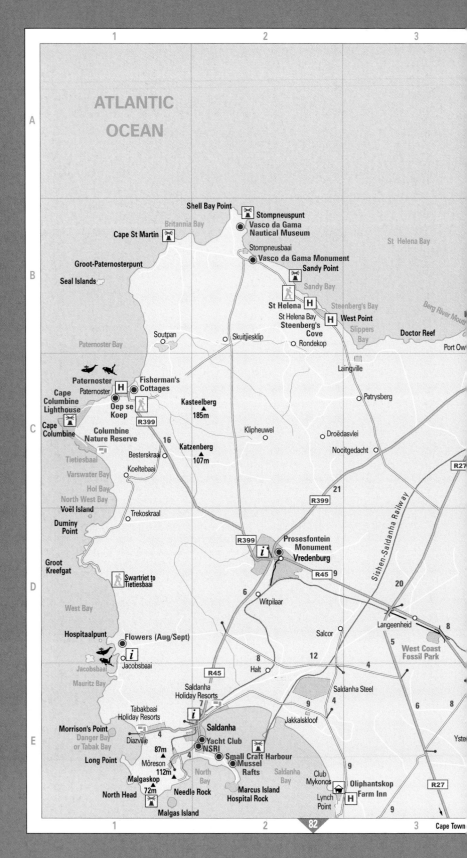

ATLANTIC
OCEAN

Shell Bay Point
Stompneuspunt
Vasco da Gama
Nautical Museum
Britannia Bay
Cape St Martin
Stompneusbaai
Vasco da Gama Monument
Groot-Paternosterpunt
Sandy Point
Seal Islands
Sandy Bay
St Helena
Steenberg's Bay
Berg River Mouth
St Helena Bay
West Point
St Helena Bay
Steenberg's
Cove
Slippers
Doctor Reef
Paternoster Bay
Soutpan
Skuitjiesklip
Rondekop
Bay
Port Ow

Laingville

Paternoster
Fisherman's
Cottages
Patrysberg
Cape
Paternoster
H
Columbine
Oep se
Kasteelberg
Lighthouse
Koep
185m
Klipheuwel
Droëdasvlei
Cape
R399
Nooitgedacht
Columbine
Columbine
16
Katzenberg
R27
Nature Reserve
107m
Besterskraal
Tietiesbaai
Koeltebaai
Varswater Bay
21
Hol Bay
North West Bay
R399
Voël Island
Trekoskraal
Duminy
Sishen-Saldanha Railway
Point
R399
Prosesfontein
Groot
Monument
20
Kreefgat
Swartriet to
Vredenburg
Tietiesbaai
R45   9
West Bay
6
Langeenheid
8
Witpilaar
West Coast
Hospitaalpunt
5
Fossil Park
Flowers (Aug/Sept)
Salcor
Jacobsbaai
i
4
Jacobsbaai
Halt
8
12
Saldanha Steel
Mauritz Bay
R45
Saldanha
Holiday Resorts
4
Tabakbaai
i
6
8
Holiday Resorts
Saldanha
Jakkalskloof
4
Morrison's Point
4
Danger Bay
Diazville
Yacht Club
or Tabak Bay
87m
NSRI
Small Craft Harbour
Yste
Long Point
Môreson
Mussel
112m
Rafts
Saldanha
Club
9
Malgaskop
North
Bay
Mykonos
Oliphantskop
72m
Marcus Island
Bay
Farm Inn
North Head
Needle Rock
Hospital Rock
Lynch
H
Point
9
Malgas Island
Cape Town

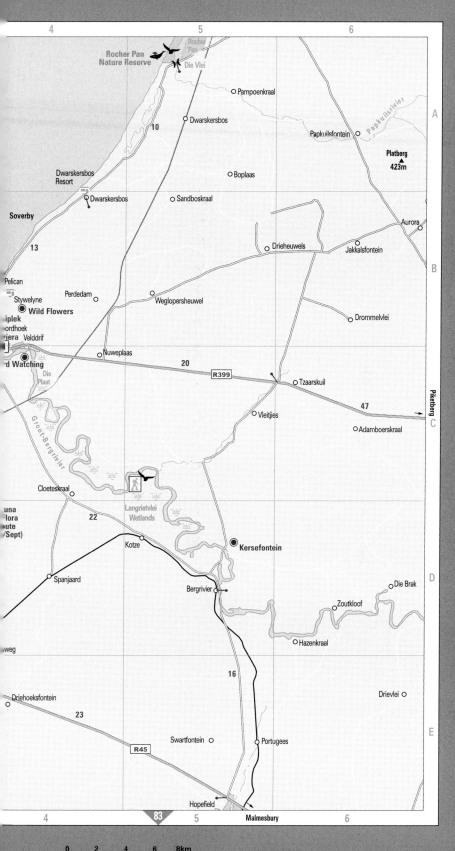

Rocher Pan
Nature Reserve

Rocher Pan

Die Vlei

Pampoenkraal

Dwarskersbos

10

Papkuilsrivier

Papkuilsfontein

Platberg
423m

Dwarskersbos
Resort

Boplaas

A

Dwarskersbos

Sandboskraal

Soverby

Aurora

13

Drieheuwels

Jakkalsfontein

B

Pelican

Stywelyne

Perdedam

Wild Flowers

Weglopersheuwel

Drommelvlei

iplek
ordhoek
iera   Velddrif

Nuweplaas

20

R399

d Watching

Die
Plaat

Tzaarskuil

Pikelberg

47

C

Vleitjies

Groot-Bergrivier

Adamboerskraal

Cloeteskraal

Langrietvlei
Wetlands

una
lora
ute
/Sept)

22

Kotze

Kersefontein

Spanjaard

Bergrivier

Die Brak

D

Zoutkloof

Hazenkraal

16

Driehoeksfontein

Drievlei

23

E

Swartfontein

Portugees

R45

Hopefield

Malmesbury

0   2   4   6   8km

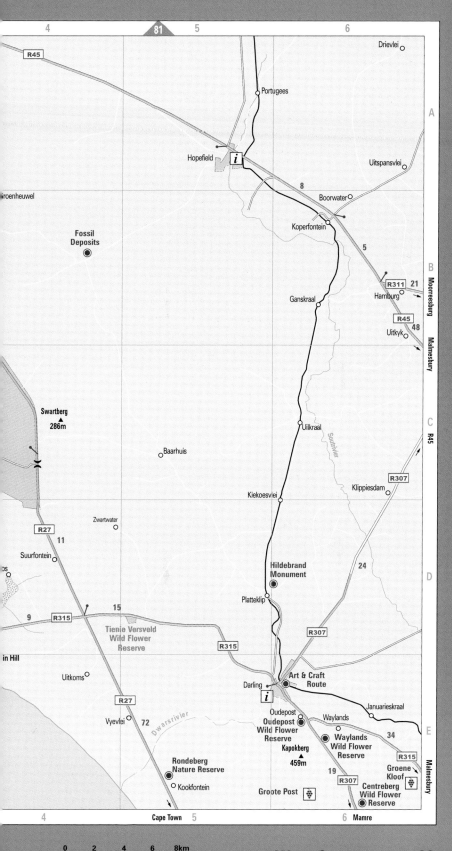

4 5 6

R45

Drievlei

Portugees

A

Hopefield *i*

8

Boorwater

Uitspansvlei

Koperfontein

Groenheuwel

5

Fossil
Deposits

B

R311 21

Hamburg

Moorreesburg

Ganskraal

R45 48

Uitkyk

Malmesbury

Swartberg
286m

C

Uilkraal

Soutrivier

R45

Baarhuis

Klippiesdam

R307

Kiekoesvlei

Zwartwater

R27

11

Hildebrand
Monument

24

D

Suurfontein

Platteklip

9 R315 15

R307

Tienie Versveld
Wild Flower
Reserve

R315

in Hill

Uitkoms

Art & Craft
Route

Darling *i*

Januarieskraal

R27

Oudepost

Waylands

Vyevlei 72

Oudepost
Wild Flower
Reserve

Waylands
Wild Flower
Reserve

34

E

Dwarsrivier

Kapokberg
459m

R315

Rondeberg
Nature Reserve

19 R307

Groene
Kloof

Malmesbury

Kookfontein

Groote Post

Centreberg
Wild Flower
Reserve

4 Cape Town 5 6 Mamre

0 2 4 6 8km

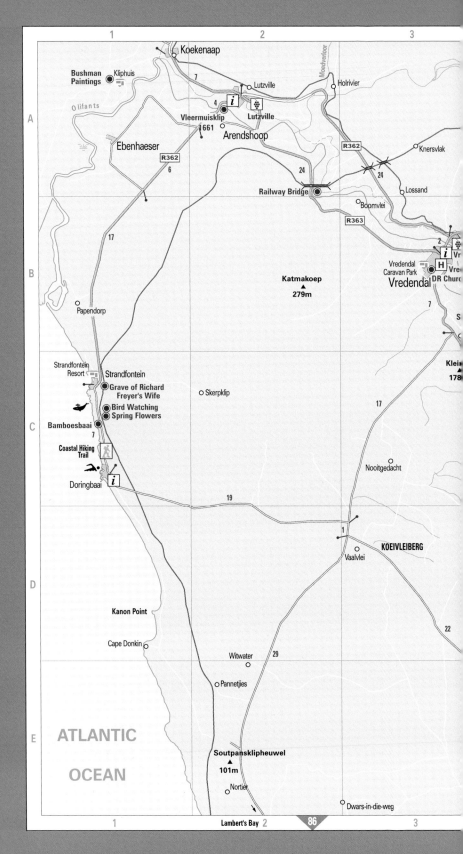

ATLANTIC

OCEAN

84   **Olifants River Valley**   Scale 1 : 300 000

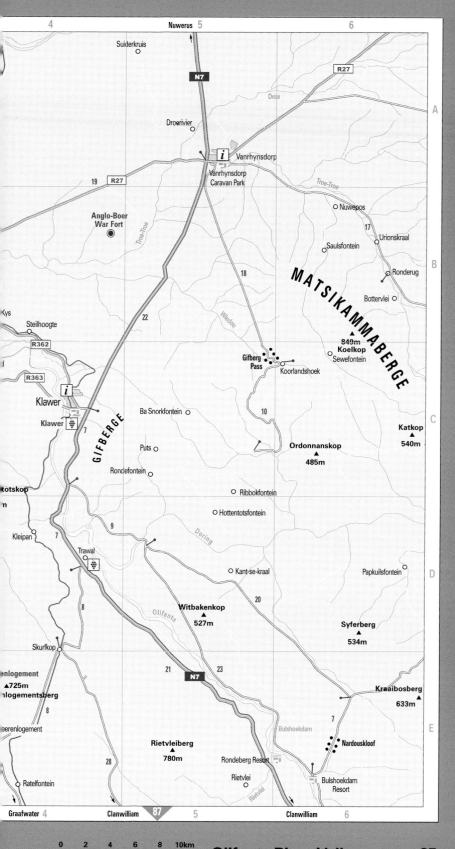

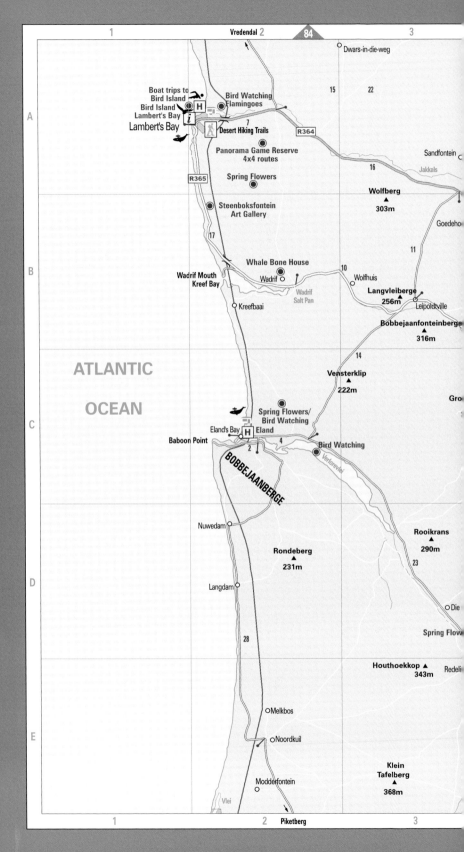

ATLANTIC

OCEAN

Dwars-in-die-weg

Boat trips to
Bird Island
Bird Island
Lambert's Bay
Lambert's Bay

**Bird Watching
Flamingoes**

Desert Hiking Trails

**Panorama Game Reserve
4x4 routes**

Spring Flowers

R364

R365

15

22

16

Jakkals

Sandfontein

Wolfberg
▲
303m

Goedeho

17

**Steenboksfontein
Art Gallery**

11

Whale Bone House

**Wadrif Mouth
Kreef Bay**

Wadrif

10

Wolfhuis

Wadrif
Salt Pan

**Langvleiberge
256m** ▲

Leipoldtville

Kreefbaai

**Bobbejaanfonteinberge
316m**

14

Vensterklip
▲
222m

Gro

**Spring Flowers/
Bird Watching**
Eland

Eland's Bay H

Baboon Point

2

4

Bird Watching

Verlorevlei

BOBBEJAANBERGE

Nuwedam

Rooikrans
▲
290m

23

Rondeberg
▲
231m

Langdam

Die

Spring Flow

28

Houthoekkop ▲
343m

Redeli

Melkbos

Noordkuil

**Klein
Tafelberg**
▲
368m

Modderfontein

Vlei

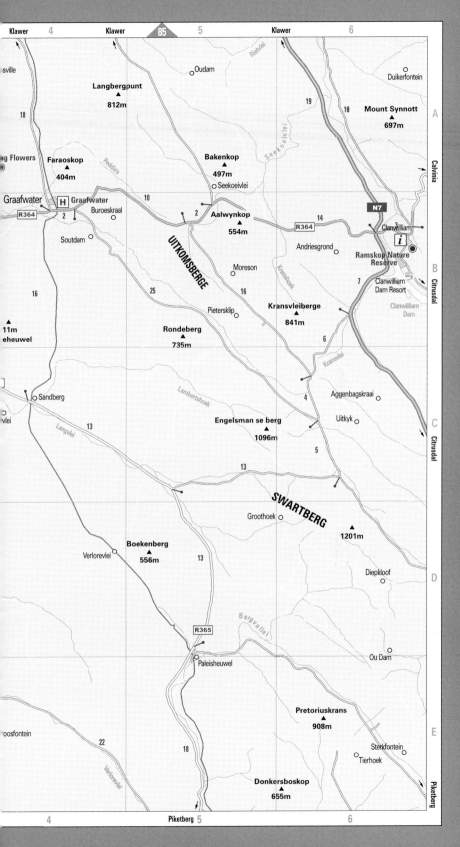

Oudam

Langbergpunt
▲
812m

Duikerfontein

19   18

Mount Synnott
▲
697m

A

18

Calvinia

sville

g Flowers

Faraoskop
▲
404m

Bakenkop
▲
497m

Seekoeivlei

Graafwater

H Graafwater

Buroeskraal

2

Aalwynkop
▲
554m

14

R364

N7

Clanwilliam

i

R364

10

Soutdam

Andriesgrond

Ramskop Nature
Reserve

B

Citrusdal

16

25

Moreson

16

Kransvleiberge
▲
841m

7

Clanwilliam
Dam Resort

Clanwilliam
Dam

11m
eheuwel

Pietersklip

Rondeberg
▲
735m

6

Kransvlei

Sandberg

Langvlei

13

Lambertshoek

4

Aggenbagskraai

Uitkyk

C

Citrusdal

vlei

Engelsman se berg
▲
1096m

5

13

Groothoek

SWARTBERG

1201m
▲

Verlorevlei

Boekenberg
▲
556m

13

Diepkloof

D

R365

Bergvallei

Paleisheuwel

Ou Dam

oosfontein

22

18

Verlorevlei

Pretoriuskrans
▲
908m

Sterkfontein

Tierhoek

E

Piketberg

Donkersboskop
▲
655m

0   2   4   6   8   10km

Olifants River Valley

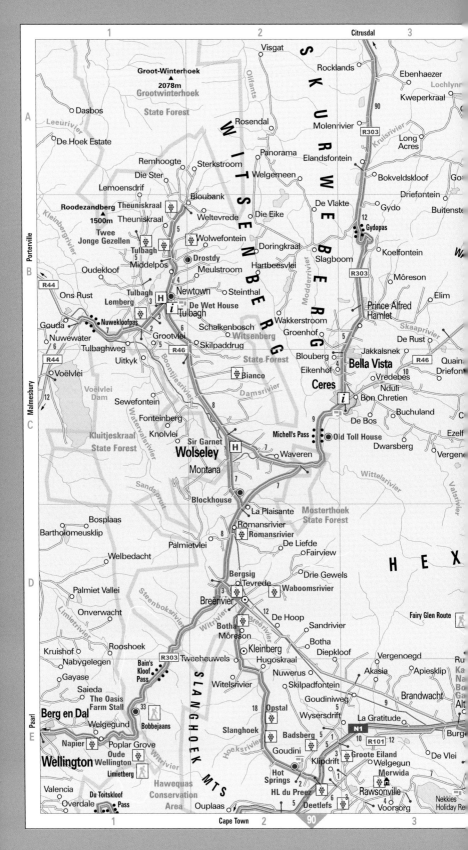

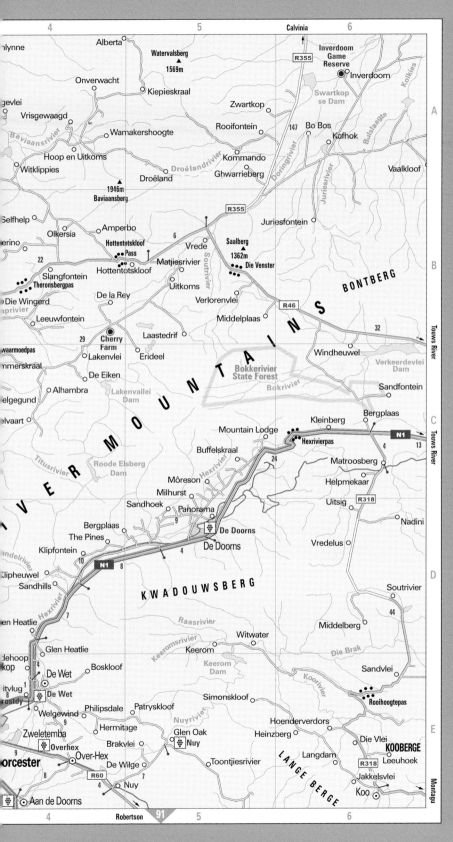

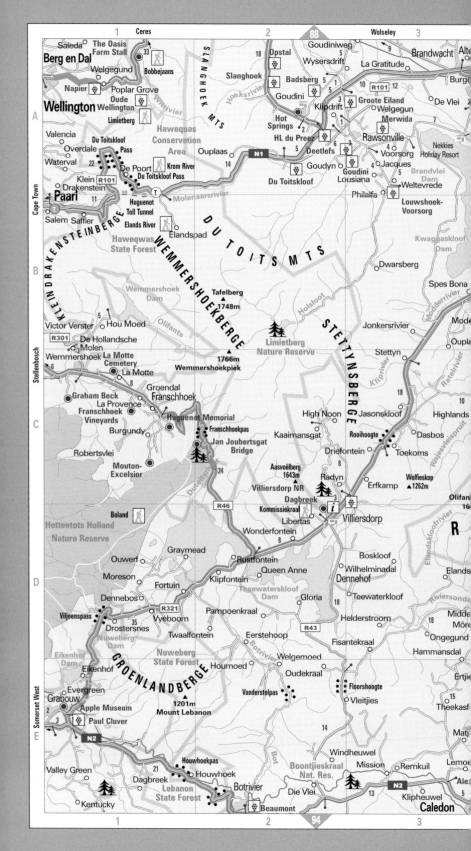

Breede River Valley

Breede River Valley Scale 1 : 340 000

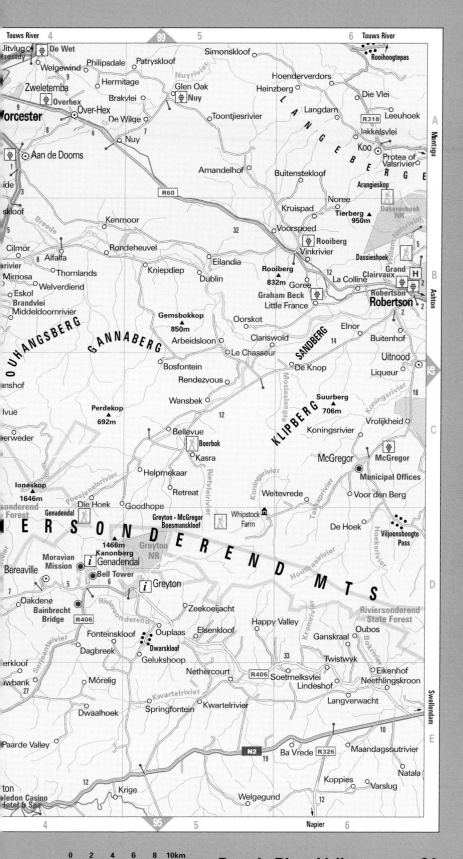

Jitvlug
rostdy
De Wet
Welgewind
Philipsdale
Patryskloof
Simonskloof
Rooihoogtepas
Hermitage
Hoenderverdors
Die Vlei
Zweletemba
Overhex
Brakvlei
Glen Oak
Nuy
Heinzberg
Langdam
Leeuhoek
R318
Worcester
Over-Hex
De Wilge
Toontjiesrivier
Jakkelsvlei
Koo
A
Nuy
Protea of
Valsrivier
Aan de Doorns
Amandelhof
Buitenstekloof
Arangieskop
ide
Noree
R60
Kruispad
Tierberg
950m
Dassieshoek
NR
skloof
Kenmoor
32
Voorspoed
Breede
Rooiberg
Vinkrivier
Dassieshoek
5
Cilmor
Rondeheuvel
Eilandia
Rooiberg
832m
La Colline
12
Grand
Clairvaux
rivier
Alfalfa
Kniepdiep
Dublin
Goree
Robertson
B
Mimosa
Thornlands
Graham Beck
Little France
Robertson
Welverdiend
Eskol
Oorskot
H
Brandvlei
Middeldoornrivier
Elnor
2
Gemsbokkop
850m
Clariswold
Buitenhof
OUHANGSBERG
GANNABERG
Arbeidsloon
SANDBERG
14
Uitnood
Le Chasseur
Bosfontein
De Knop
Liqueur
92
anshof
Rendezvous
Suurberg
706m
18
lvue
Wansbek
Koningsrivier
Vrolijkheid
erweder
12
Perdekop
692m
Bellevue
Boerbok
C
Kasra
Koningsrivier
Ionaskop
1646m
Helpmekaar
McGregor
McGregor
onderend
Forest
Retreat
Weltevrede
Municipal Offices
Die Hoek
Goodhope
Voor den Berg
Genadendal
Greyton - McGregor
Boesmanskloof
Whipstock
Farm
De Hoek
Viljoenshoogte
Pass
Bereaville
1466m
Kanonberg
Greyton
NR
Moravian
Mission
Genadendal
E R S O N D E R E N D   M T S
Bell Tower
7
Oakdene
Bainbrecht
Bridge
R406
Greyton
Zeekoeijacht
Riviersonderend
State Forest
Fonteinskloof
Ouplaas
Elsenkloof
Happy Valley
Oubos
D
erkloof
Dagbreek
Dwarskloof
Gelukshoop
Nethercourt
33
Twistwyk
Gemskraal
Eikenhof
Neethlingskroon
wbank
27
Môrelig
R406
Soetmelksvlei
Lindeshof
Kwartelrivier
Dwaalhoek
Springfontein
Kwartelrivier
Langverwacht
Paarde Valley
10
E
N2
Ba Vrede
R326
Maandagsoutrivier
19
Natala
ton
ledon Casino
otel & Spa
12
Krige
Koppies
Varslug
Welgegund
12

0   2   4   6   8   10km

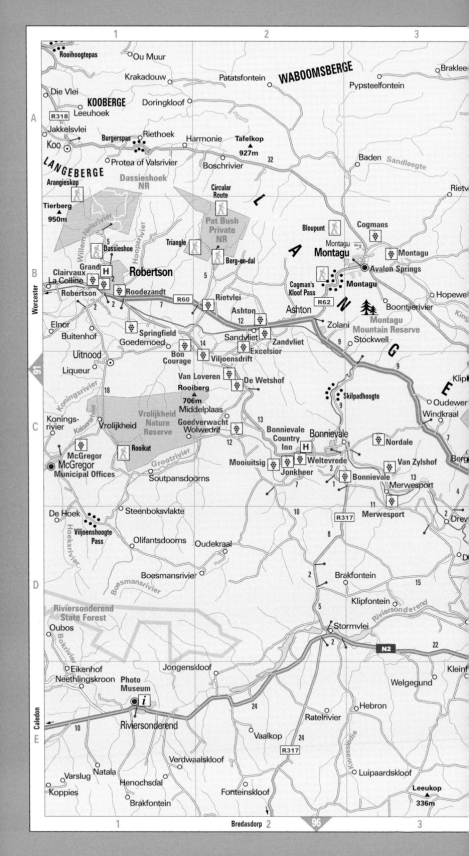

Breede River Valley

Scale 1 : 340 000

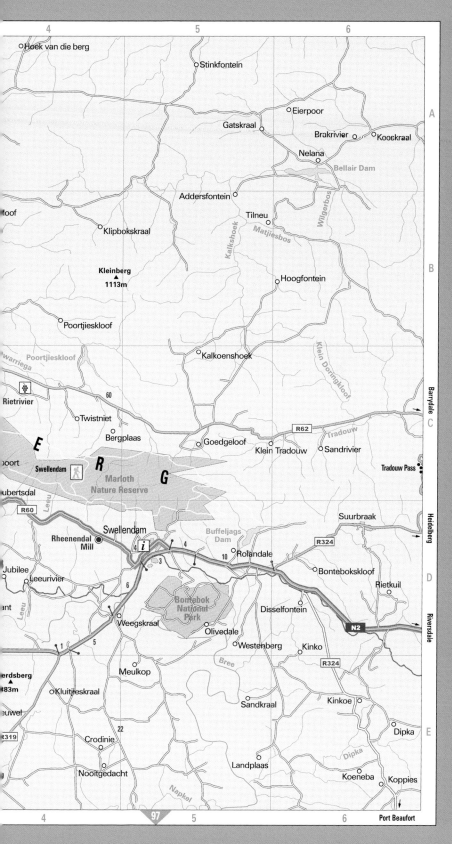

Breede River Valley

0 2 4 6 8 10km

ATLANTIC
OCEAN

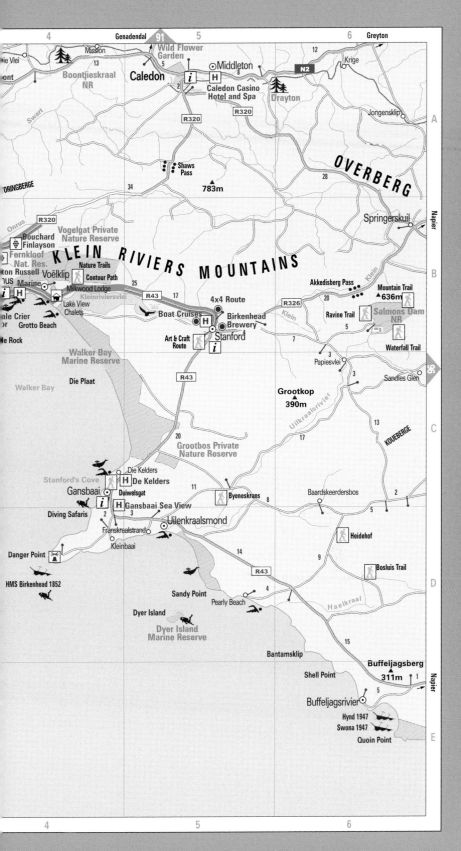

4   5   6   Greyton

Mission
Wild Flower Garden
ie Vlei
Middleton
Krige
Boontjieskraal NR
Caledon
Jongensklip
N2
Caledon Casino Hotel and Spa
Drayton

R320

R320

A

Napier

O V E R B E R G

Shaws Pass
ORINGBERGE
783m
28
34

Springerskuil

R320
Bouchard Finlayson
Vogelgat Private Nature Reserve
Onrus

K L E I N R I V I E R S M O U N T A I N S

Fernkloof Nat. Res.
Nature Trails
ton Russell
Voëlklip
Contour Path
Akkedisberg Pass
Mountain Trail
636m
B
NUS Marine
Milkwood Lodge
25
20
Salmons Dam NR
Kleinriviersvlei
R43
17
4x4 Route
R326
ale Crier
Lake View Chalets
Boat Cruises
Birkenhead Brewery
Ravine Trail
Waterfall Trail
Grotto Beach
Art & Craft Route
Stanford
7
le Rock

Walker Bay Marine Reserve
Klein
5
Papiesvlei
3
Sandies Glen

Die Plaat
R43
Walker Bay
Grootkop
390m
3
13
KOUEBERGE
C

20
Grootbos Private Nature Reserve
17

Die Kelders
Stanford's Cove
De Kelders
11
Byeneskrans
Baardskeerdersbos
2
Gansbaai
Duiwelsgat
8
5
Diving Safaris
Gansbaai Sea View
Franskraalstrand
Uilenkraalsmond
Heidehof
Kleinbaai
14
9
Danger Point
Bosluis Trail
R43
4
D
HMS Birkenhead 1852
Sandy Point
Pearly Beach
Haelkraal
Dyer Island
Dyer Island Marine Reserve
15
Bantamsklip

Buffeljagsberg
311m
1
Shell Point
Napier
5
Buffeljagsrivier
Hynd 1947
Swona 1947
Quoin Point
E

0 2 4 6 8 10km

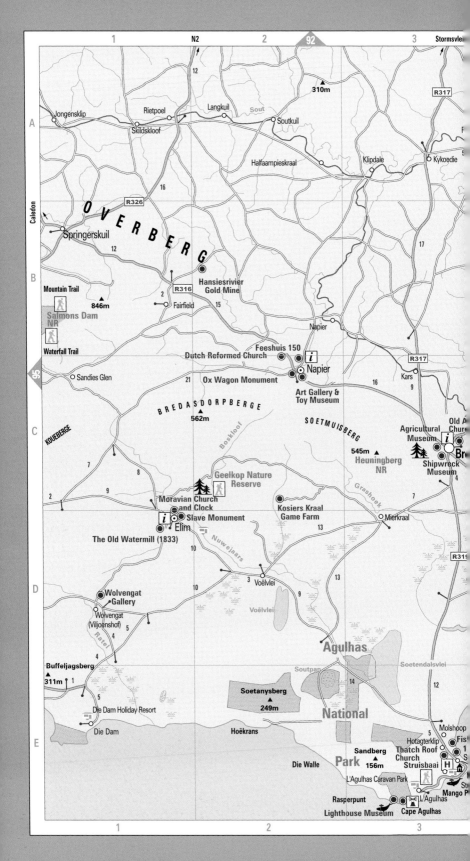

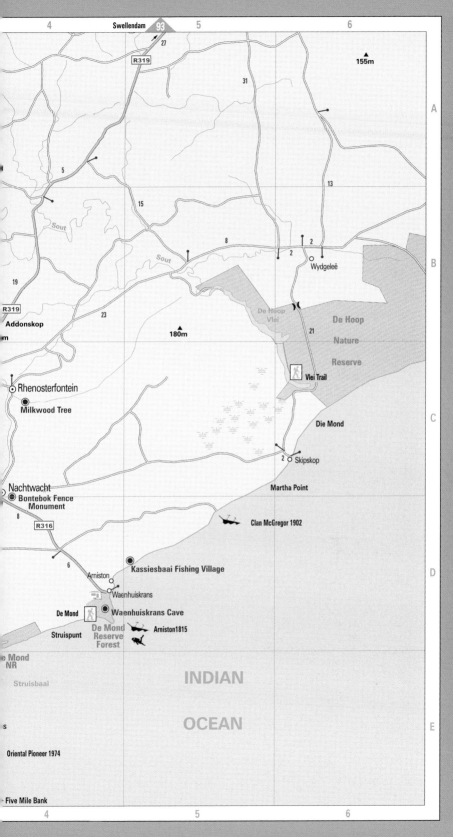

27

R319

31

155m

4

5

6

A

5

15

13

Sout

Sout

8

2

2

Wydgeleë

B

19

R319

23

De Hoop
Vlei

De Hoop

Addonskop

m

180m

21

Nature

Reserve

Rhenosterfontein

Vlei Trail

Milkwood Tree

Die Mond

C

2

Skipskop

Nachtwacht

Martha Point

Bontebok Fence
Monument

8

Clan McGregor 1902

R316

6

Kassiesbaai Fishing Village

Arniston

D

Waenhuiskrans

De Mond

Waenhuiskrans Cave

De Mond
Reserve
Forest

Arniston1815

Struispunt

e Mond
NR

INDIAN

Struisbaai

s

OCEAN

E

Oriental Pioneer 1974

Five Mile Bank

4

5

6

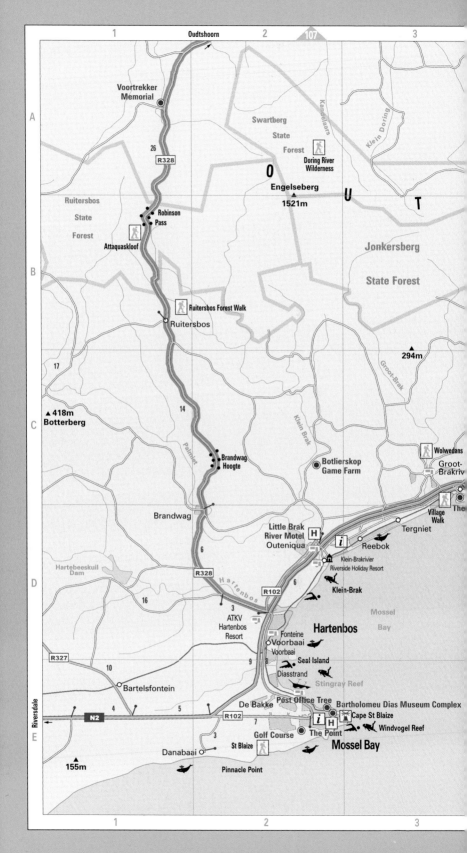

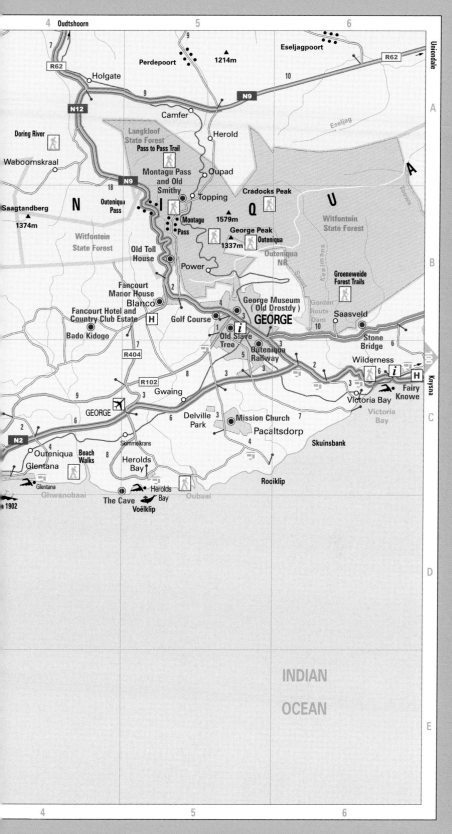

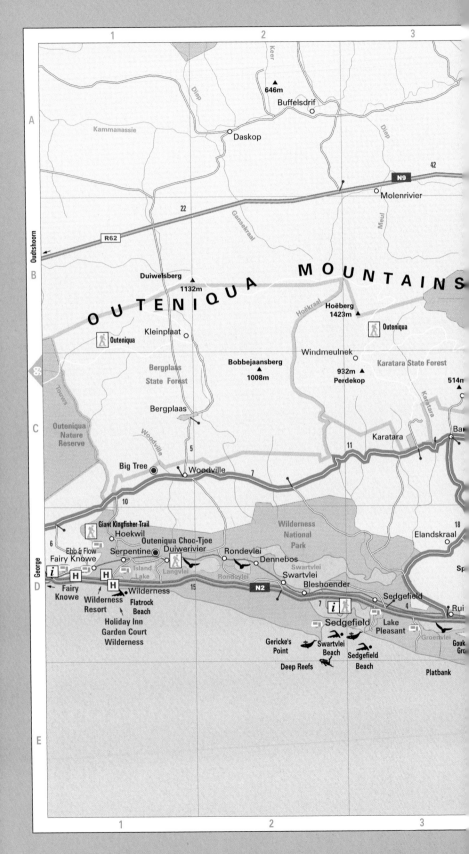

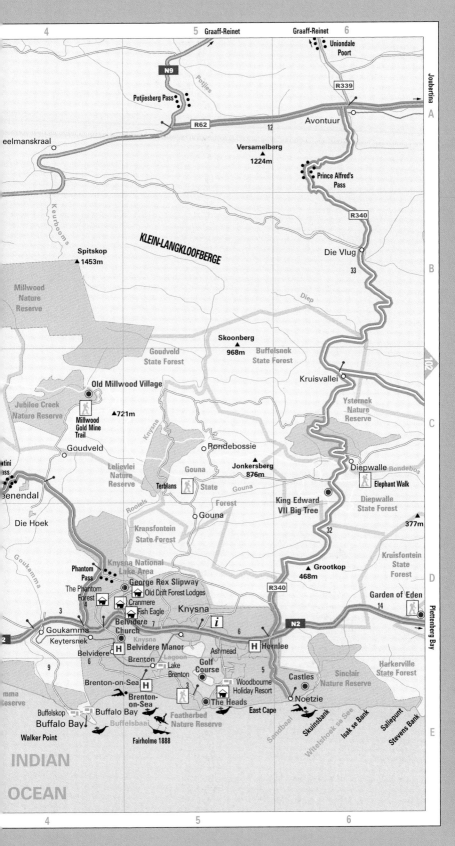

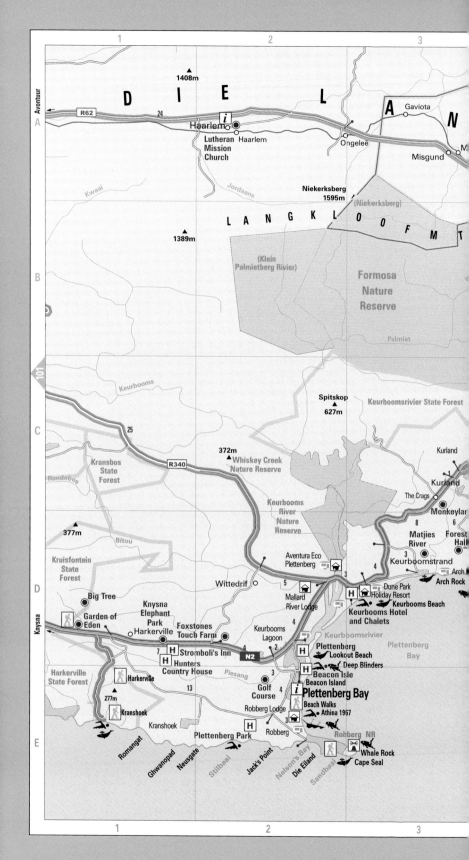

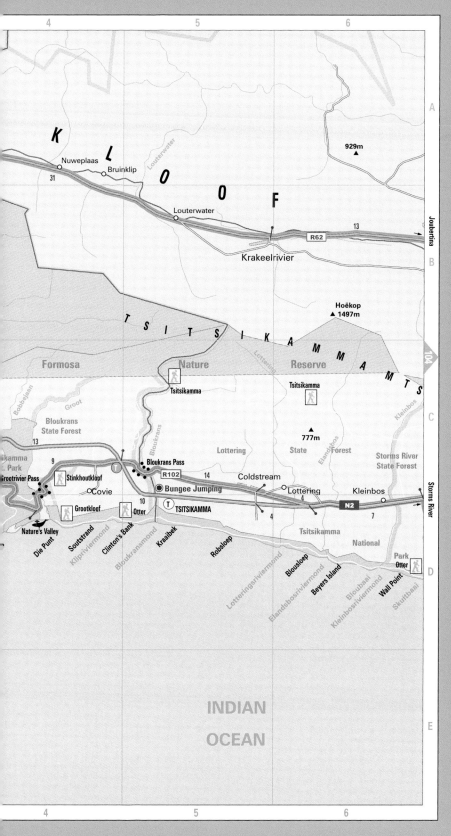

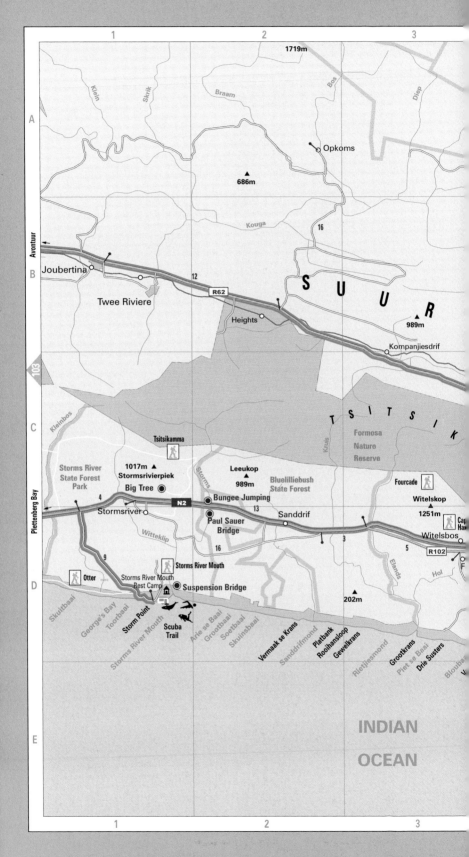

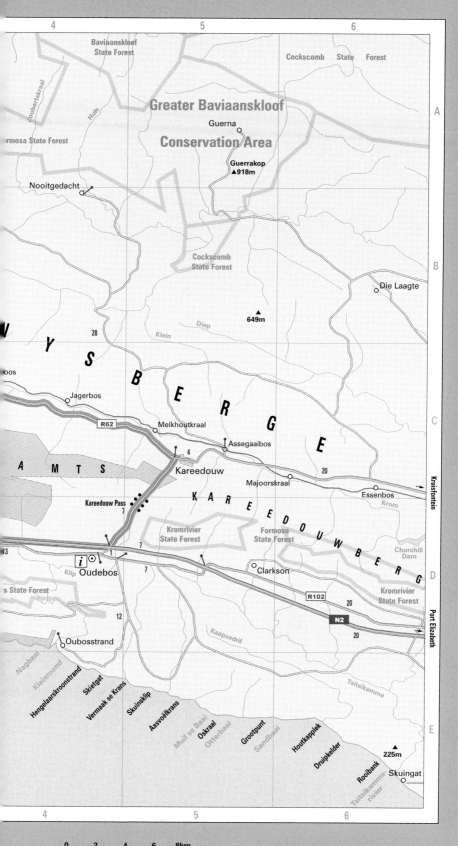

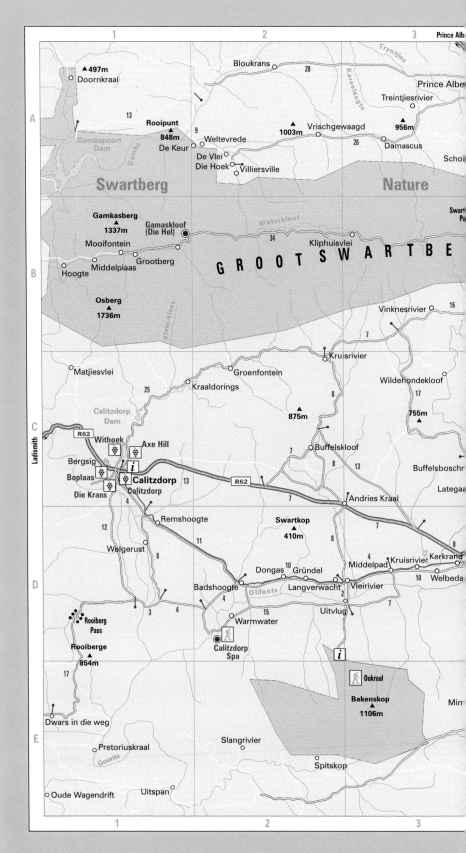

Scale 1 : 350 000

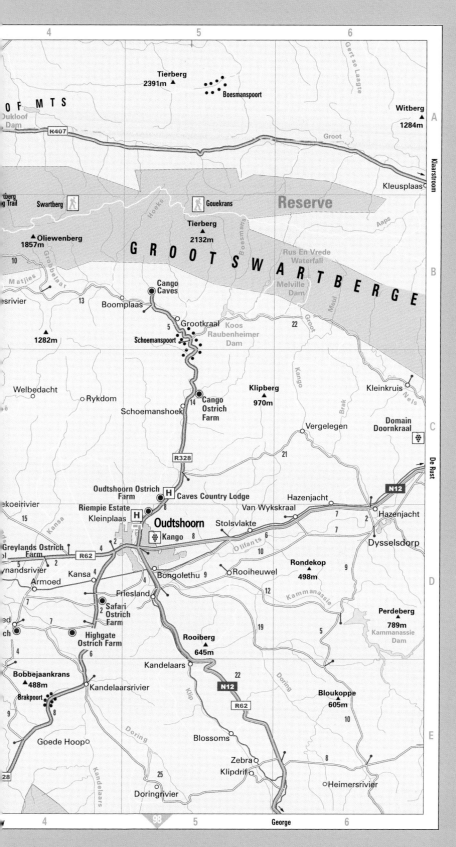

Index Index Index Index Index In

WESTERN CAPE CONTACT DETAILS & INFORMATION

The following telephone numbers (and cyber connections) are correct at time of going to print. Numbers and codes do change over time, as do the names of establishments. For any queries dial 1023 (telephone enquiries), 10118 (the Talking Yellow Pages) or visit ww.yellowpages.co.za (the electronic yellow pages).
NOTE: numbers listed are all phone numbers – no fax numbers or physical addresses are provided here. World-wide web addresses are listed as ww for space purposes).

EMERGENCIES
Ambulance 10177
Fire and other emergencies 107
Automobile Association Emergency
0800 01 01 01

GENERAL
South Africa online: ww.southafrica.net
Western Cape Tourism Board
021 426 5639, info@capetourism.org,
ww.capetourism.org
Cape Town Tourism Board 021 426 4260,
info@cape-town.org, ww.cape-town.org
Weather Bureau 082 162
Cape Town International Airport 021 937 1200
George Airport 044 876 9310

TRANSPORT
Automobile Association 0800 01 01 01
Spoornet 086 000 8888
Blue Train 021 449 2672
Metrorail 0800 65 64 63

BUS SERVICES
Greyhound 021 505 63 63
Intercape 0861 28 72 87
Translux 021 449 3333

CAR RENTAL
Avis 0861 02 11 11
Budget 0861 01 66 22
Imperial 0861 13 10 00
Tempest 021 424 5000
National Car Rental 0800 011 323

ACCOMMODATION
City Lodge 0800 11 37 90
Holiday Inn 0800 11 77 11
Protea Hotels 0861 11 90 00
Southern Sun 0800 11 77 11

AIRLINES
British Airways 0860 01 1747
KLM 0860 24 77 47
Kulula.com 0861 58 58 52
Nationwide 021 936 2050
South African Airways 021 936 1111

MONEY MATTERS
ABSA 0800 111 155
American Express 0800 11 09 29
Diners Club 0860 34 63 77
First National Bank 0800 110 132
Mastercard 0800 990 418
Nedbank 0800 110 929
Rennies Foreign Exchange (Thomas Cook)
021 418 3744
Standard Bank 0800 020 600
VISA 0800 990 475

CELLPHONE PROVIDERS
Cell C 0860 08 40 84
MTN 083 173
Vodacom 082 111

ENTERTAINMENT
Artscape Theatre Centre 021 421 7695
Baxter Theatre Centre 021 685 7800
Computicket 083 915 8000
Nu-Metro 0861 10 02 20
On Broadway 021 418 8338
Ster-Kinekor 0860 30 02 22

CAPE TOWN
Cape Town Tourism Board 021 426 4260,
info@cape-town.org, ww.cape-town.org

CAPE TOWN CITY BOWL & ENVIRONS
Cape Town Holocaust Centre 021 462 5553,
Cape Town International Convention Centre
021 410 5000
Castle of Good Hope 021 787 1249
District Six Museum 021 461 8745
IMAX movie theatre 021 419 7365
The Mount Nelson Hotel 021 483 1000
Planetarium 021 481 3900
Radisson Hotel, Granger Bay 021 418 5729
Robben Island 021 419 1300
SA Museum 021 481 3800
South African National Gallery 021 467 4660
St George's Cathedral 021 424 7360
Table Mountain Aerial Cableway 021 424 8181
Two Oceans Aquarium 021 418 3823
V&A Waterfront 021 408 7600

112

THE CAPE PENINSULA
Blaauwberg Tourism Bureau 021 557 8600,
btb@blaauwberg.co.za,
ww.blaauwberg.net/tourisminfo
Cape of Good Hope Nature Reserve
021 780 9204
Cape Peninsula National Parks 021 780 9100
Cape Point Ostrich Farm 021 780 9294
Grass Roots 021 706 1006
Legend Tours 021 697 4056
Peninsula Tourism 021 788 6193,
peninsulatourism@yebo.co.za
The Two Oceans Restaurant 021 780 9200
Tygerberg Tourism 021 970 3172,
tourism@tygerberg.gov.za
Western Cape Action Tours 021 461 1371

Camps Bay
Bay Hotel 021 430 4444
Blues Restaurant 021 438 2040
Theatre on the Bay 021 438 3301

Constantia
Buitenverwachting 021 794 5191
Constantia Uitsig 021 794 1810
Constantia Village Shopping Centre
021 794 5065
Groot Constantia 021 794 5128
Klein Constantia 021 794 5188
Jonkershuis 021 794 6255
Peninsula Tourism (Constantia) 021 762 0687,
pencon@yebo.co.za
Steenberg Estate 021 713 2211

Durbanville (Tygerberg)
Altydgedacht 021 976 1295
Bloemendal Wines 021 976 2682
Diemersdal Wines 021 976 3361
Durbanville Hills winery 021 558 1300
GrandWest Casino and Entertainment World
021 505 7777
Meerendal Estate 021 975 1655
N1 City shopping centre 021 595 1170
Nitida Estate 021 976 1467
Tygerberg Nature Reserve 021 913 5695
Tygerberg Tourism 021 914 1786,
tourism@tygerberg.gov.za
Tyger Valley Shopping Centre 021 914 1822
Tygerberg Zoo 021 884 4494

Fish Hoek
Peninsula Tourism (Fish Hoek) 021 782 4531,
jhw24t@absamail.co.za,
www.fishhoekvalley.co.za

Hout Bay
Chapman's Peak Hotel 021 790 1036
Mariner's Wharf 021 790 1100
Peninsula Tourism (Hout Bay) 021 790 1264,
penhout@yebo.co.za, ww.houtbay.org
World of Birds 021 790 2730

Kalk Bay
Cape to Cuba 021 788 1566
Kalk Bay Harbour 021 788 8313
Olympia Bakery 021 788 6396

Kommetjie
Imhoff Farm 021 789 1711
Peninsula Tourism (Kommetjie) 021 783 4545

Melkbosstrand / Milnerton
Canal Walk Shopping Centre 021 555 0558
Koeberg Nuclear Power Station 021 550 4021
Ratanga Junction 0861 200 300

Muizenberg
Natale Labia Museum 021 788 4106
Peninsula Tourism (Muizenberg) 021 788 6176,
penmuiz@yebo.co.za

Newlands
Cavendish Square Shopping Centre
021 671 8042
Kirstenbosch National Botanical Garden
021 799 8783
South African Breweries 021 658 7386

Noordhoek
Peninsula Tourism (Noordhoek) 021 789 2812,
info@noordhoektourism.co.za,
ww.noordhoektourism.co.za

Simon's Town
Boulders Beach 021 701 8692
Peninsula Tourism (Simon's Town)
021 786 5798
The Residency Museum 021 786 3046
South African naval base 021 787 3911
Warrior Toy Museum 021 786 1395

THE WINELANDS
Helderberg Tourism Bureau 021 851 4022,
info@helderbergtourism.co.za,
ww.helderbergtourism.co.za
Winelands Regional Tourism Office 021 872
0686, info@capewinelands.org,
ww.capewinelands.org

Gordon's Bay, Strand & Somerset West
Helderberg Tourism Bureau 021 851 4022,
info@helderbergtourism.co.za,
ww.helderbergtourism.co.za
Monkey Town 021 858 1060
Somerset Mall Shopping Centre 021 852 7114
Vergelegen 021 847 1334

Franschhoek
Boschendal Estate 021 870 4200
Haute Cabrière 021 876 3688
Franschhoek Tourism Bureau 021 876 3603,
info@franschhoek.org.za,
ww.franschhoek.org.za

Franschhoek Wine Route (Vignerons de Franschhoek) 021 876 3603
Huguenot Museum 021 876 2532
La Motte 021 876 3114
La Petite Ferme 021 876 3016
Môreson Estate 021 876 3055

Paarl
Afrikaans Language Museum 021 872 3441
Butterfly World 021 875 5628
Crocodile Farm 021 863 1142
Fairview Wine Estate 021 863 2450
KWV (HO & Wine Emporium) 021 807 3007
Nederburg 021 862 3104
Paarl Museum 021 872 2651
Paarl Tourism Bureau 021 872 3829,
paarl@cis.co.za, ww.paarlonline.com

Stellenbosch
Bergkelder 021 809 7000
Delheim 021 888 4600
Historical Walks 021 883 9633
Morgenhof 021 889 5510
Oom Samie se Winkel 021 887 0797
Spier 021 8091100
Stellenbosch Information Office 021 883 3584,
eikestad@iafrica.com, ww.istellenbosch.org.za
Stellenbosch Museum 021 887 2902
Stellenbosch University 021 808 4515
Stellenbosch Wine Route 021 886 4310
Van Rhyn Brandy Cellars 021 881 3875

Wellington
Hottentots Holland Nature Reserve
028 840 4826
SAD (Wellington Fruit Growers) 021 864 8690
Wellington Museum 021 873 4710
Wellington Tourism Bureau 021 873 4604,
welltour@mweb.co.za, ww.visitwellington.com
Wellington Wine Route 021 873 4604

WEST COAST, OVERBERG, KAROO AND GARDEN ROUTE
Breede River Valley Tourism 023 347 6411,
manager@breederivervalley.co.za,
ww.breederivervalley.co.za
Central Karoo Regional Tourism Office
023 449 1000, karootour@internext.co.za,
ww.centralkaroo.co.za
The Garden Route Klein Karoo Regional Tourism
Organization 044 873 6314,
info@gardenroute.org.za,
ww.capegardenroute.org
Hex River Valley Tourism 023 356 2041,
grapeescape@mweb.co.za
Overberg Tourism 028 214 1466,
info@capeoverberg.org, ww.capeoverberg.org
West Coast Regional Tourism 022 433 2380,
tourism@capewestcoast.org,
ww.capewestcoast.org

Arniston
Arniston Hotel 028 445 9000
Tourist Info 028 424 2584,
suidpunt@brd.dorea.co.za, ww.capeagulhas.info

Barrydale
Tourist Info 028 572 1572,
info@barrydale.co.za, ww.barrydale.co.za

Beaufort West
Karoo National Park 023 415 2828
Beaufort West Tourism 023 415 1488,
bwtbinfo@xsinet.co.za,
ww.beaufortwestsa.co.za

Bredasdorp
De Hoop Nature Reserve 028 425 5020
Tourist Info 028 424 2584,
suidpunt@brd.dorea.co.za, ww.capeagulhas.info
Shipwreck Museum 028 424 1240

Caledon
De Overberger Hotel 028 214 1271
Tourist Info 028 212 1511,
calmuse@intekom.co.za

Ceres
The Fruit Route 083 363 1719
Kagga Kamma Nature Reserve 021 872 4343
Matroosberg Reserve 023 312 2282
Togryers Museum (Transport Riders' Museum)
023 312 2045
Tourist Info 023 316 1287, info@ceres.org.za,
ww.ceres.org.za

Citrusdal
Tourist Info 022 921 3210, info@citrusdal.info,
ww.citrusdal.info

Clanwilliam
Cederberg Wines 027 482 2827
Cederberg Wilderness Area & Nature Reserve
027 482 2812
Die Kunshuis Art Gallery 027 482 1940
Rooibos Ltd. – Tea & Natural Products
027 482 2155
Tourist Info 027 482 2024,
cederberg@lando.co.za, ww.clanwilliam.info

Darling
Evita se Perron 022 492 2831
Rondeberg Nature Reserve 022 492 3099
Tourist Info 022 492 3361,
darlinginfo@mweb.co.za,
ww.darlingtourism.co.za
Wild Flower Line 022 433 2380

Dwarskersbos
Tourist Info 022 783 1821

Eland's Bay
Sea Fisheries - crayfish permits 022 972 1720
Tourist Info 022 972 1640,
info@elandsbay.co.za, ww.elandsbay.co.za

Elgin / Grabouw
Elgin Apple Museum 021 848 9060
Paul Cluver Amphitheatre 021 844 0506
Tourist Info 021 848 9838

Elim
Tourist Info 028 482 1806

George
George Museum 044 873 5343
Fancourt Hotel and Country Club
044 804 0000
Outeniqua Choo-Tjoe 044 801 8288
Outeniqua Nature Reserve 044 870 8323
Outeniqua Railway Museum 044 801 8264
Tourist Info 044 801 9295,
info@georgetourism.co.za,
ww.georgetourism.co.za

Greyton
Greyton Lodge 028 254 9876
Greyton Nature Reserve 028 254 9414
The Post House 028 254 9995
Tourist Info 028 254 9414, alblain@iafrica.com,
ww.greyton.net

Hermanus
Bouchard Finlayson Vineyards 028 312 3515
Hamilton Russell Vineyards 028 312 3595
Hermanus Whale Hotline 028 312 2629
Old Harbour Museum 028 312 1475
Tourist Info 028 312 2629,
infoburo@hermanus.co.za, ww.hermanus.co.za

Hopefield
Tourist Info 022 723 0500,
ninettel@saldanhabay.co.za

Jacobsbaai
Tourist Info 022 714 2088,
bureau@kingsley.co.za, ww.capewestcoast.org

Kleinplasie
Kleinplasie Living Open Air Museum
023 342 2225

Kleinmond
Tourist Info 028 271 5657,
info@ecoscape.org.za, ww.ecoscape.org.za

Knysna
Featherbed Nature Reserve 044 382 1693
Knysna Forest 044 382 5466
Knysna Oyster Co. 044 382 6941
Knysna Quays Waterfront 044 382 0955
Mitchell's Brewery 044 382 4685
Nature's Valley 042 280 3561

Outeniqua Choo-Tjoe 044 801 8288
Tourist Info 044 382 5510,
knysna.tourism@pixie.co.za,
ww.knysna-info.co.za

Laingsburg
Tourist Info 023 551 1019

Lambert's Bay
Tourist Info 027 432 1000,
lambertsinfo@mweb.co.za

Langebaan
Club Mykonos 022 707 7000
Die Strandloper 022 772 2490
Postberg Nature Reserve 022 772 2144
Tourist Info 022 772 1515, lbninfo@mweb.co.za,
ww.langebaaninfo.com
West Coast Fossil Park 022 766 1606
West Coast National Park 022 772 2144
Wild Flower line 022 433 2380

Malmesbury
Bokomo Mills 022 487 2240
Malmesbury Museum 022 482 2332
Riverlands Nature Reserve 022 487 7360
Swartland Wine Route 022 487 1133
Tourist Info 022 487 1133,
swartlandinfo@westc.co.za,
ww.capewestcoast.org

Matjiesfontein
Lord Milner Hotel 023 561 3011

McGregor
Tourist Info 023 625 1954,
mcgregortour@telkomsa.net,
ww.mcgregor.org.za
Vrolijkheid Nature Reserve 023 625 1621

Montagu
Montagu Hot Mineral Springs 023 614 1050
Montagu Museum 023 614 1950
Tourist Info 023 614 2471,
info@montagu-ashton.info,
ww.montagu-ashton.info

Mossel Bay
Tourist Info 044 690 3077,
iti26050@mweb.co.za,
ww.capegardenroute.org/mbay

Oudtshoorn
CP Nel Museum 044 272 7306
Cango Caves 044 272 7410
Cango Ostrich Farm 044 272 4623
Cango Wildlife Ranch 044 272 5593
Swartberg Nature Reserve and Pass
044 279 2746
Tourist Info 044 279 2532, otb@mweb.co.za,
ww.oudtshoorn.com

Paternoster
Cape Columbine Lighthouse 022 752 2705
Columbine Nature Reserve 022 752 2718
Tourist Info 022 715 1142, tour@mailbox.co.za

Piketberg
Historic Watermill 022 913 1947
Piketberg Museum 022 913 1126
Tourist Info 022 913 2063,
pikettourism@telkomsa.net, ww.piketberg.com
Winkelshoek Wine Cellar 022 913 1092

Plettenberg Bay
Goukamma Nature Reserve 044 383 0042
Nature Conservation & Reserves 044 533 2125
Tourist Info 044 533 4065,
info@plettenbergbay.co.za,
ww.plettenbergbay.co.za

Porterville
Agri Tourism 022 931 2134
Groot Winterhoek Nature Reserve
022 931 2900
Tourist Info 022 931 3732,
pvilletourism@mbury.new.co.za,
ww.capewestcoast.org

Port Owen
Port Owen Marina 022 783 1144
Tourist Info 022 783 1821
West Coast Art Gallery 022 783 1118

Prince Albert
Tourist Info 023 541 1366,
princealberttourism@intekom.co.za,
ww.patourism.co.za

Robertson
Dassieshoek Nature Reserve 023 615 1100
De Wetshof 023 615 1853
Graham Beck 023 626 1214
Kolgans River Cruise Restaurant 023 626 2012
Robertson Museum 023 626 3681
Robertson Wine Route 023 626 3167
Sheilam Cactus Farm 023 626 4133
Soekershof (world's largest maze)
023 626 4134
Tourist Info 023 626 4437,
info@robertson.org

Saldanha
SAS Saldanha Nature Reserve 022 702 3523
Tourist Info 022 714 2088,
bureau@kingsley.co.za,
ww.capewestcoast.org

Sedgefield
Goukamma Nature Reserve 044 383 0042
Tourist Info 044 343 2658,
sedgebiz@isat.co.za

St Helena
Tourist Info 022 715 1142, tour@mailbox.co.za
Vasco da Gama Nautical Museum
022 742 1906

Stilbaai
Tourist Info 028 754 2549,
infosb@telkomsa.co.za,

Swellendam
Bontebok National Park 028 514 2735
Hermitage Liqueur Farm 028 514 3132
The Drostdy Museum 028 514 1138
Marloth Nature Reserve 028 514 1410
Tourist Info 028 514 2770,
infoswd@sdm.dorea.co.za
ww.swellendamtourism.co.za

Tulbagh
Tourist Info 023 230 1348

Vanrhynsdorp
Kokerboom Succulent Nursery 027 219 1062
Latsky Radio Museum Tel 027 219 1032
San Rock Painting tours 027 219 1555
Tourist Info 027 219 1552,
vanrhynsdorp@kingsley.co.za,
ww.vanrhynsorp.org

Velddrif
Tourist Info 022 783 1821

Vredenburg
Vredenburg Golf Course 022 715 3003
Tourist Info 022 715 1142, tour@mailbox.co.za

Vredendal
Matzikama Eco Park 027 213 2253
Spuitdrift Wine Cellar 027 213 3086
Tourist Info 027 213 3678
Vredendal Co-op 027 213 1080

Wilderness
Eco-Tourism Association 044 877 0045,
weta@wildernessinfo.co.za,
ww.wildernessinfo.co.za

Witsand
Tourist Info 028 537 1010, info@witsand.com,
ww.witsand.com

Worcester
Karoo National Botanic Garden 023 347 0785
Tourist Info 023 348 2795,
ww.breedevalley.co.za

Wuppertal
Tourist Info 027 492 3410

Yzerfontein
Tourist Info 022 451 2366